INSIDE Essays

INSIDE Essays

Douglas Hilker

Harcourt Canada

Orlando Austin New York San Diego Toronto London

Canadian Cataloguing in Publication Data
Main entry under title:

Inside Essays I

ISBN 0-7747-1400-X

1. Canadian essays (English) - 20th century.
2. American essays - 20th century. I. Hilker, Douglas

PS8373.I67 1992   C814'.5408   C92-093669-5
PR9197.7.I67 1992

Cover Art: *Rob Johannsen*
Title Logotype/Design: *Barry Lavender*

Illustrations
Rob Johannsen

Photographs
p. 43 J. A. Wilkinson/Valan Photos; pp. 84–85 J. Blank/H. Armstrong/
Comstock; pp. 116–117 Richard Harrington/Comstock; p. 140 Dorothy
Haegert/Arsenal Pulp Press 1989; pp. 224 –225 (*clockwise from bottom left*)
W. P. Whittman/Comstock, Colin Quirk/Comstock, George
Hunter/Comstock, National Archives Canada PA184047, John
Fulker/Comstock.

 This book is printed on acid-free paper.

Printed in Canada
3 4 5   06 05 04

Douglas Hilker
English Department Head, Runnymede Collegiate Institute,
City of York Board of Education
A teacher with twenty-six years of experience, Douglas is also one
of the authors of the *Your Voice and Mine* series. His belief that the
classroom should echo the students' world is evident in his choice
of essays selected for *Inside Essays I* and *II*.

The author and publisher gratefully acknowledge the following
educators for their evaluation and suggestions:

Elizabeth Eisner, English Teacher,
David Thompson Secondary School,
Vancouver, British Columbia

Graham Foster, Language Arts Supervisor,
Calgary Catholic School Board,
Calgary, Alberta

Carl Horak, English Teacher,
Father Lacombe High School,
Calgary, Alberta

Gillda Leitenberg, Associate Professor, Faculty of Education,
York University,
North York, Ontario

Lyle Meeres, English Department Head,
Lindsay Thurber Comprehensive High School,
Red Deer, Alberta

Sharon O'Byrne, English Department Head,
F. W. Johnson Collegiate,
Regina, Saskatchewan

Penny Thacker, English Consultant,
The York Region Board of Education,
Aurora, Ontario

Terry Wadden, English Department Head,
Millwood High School,
Lower Sackville, Nova Scotia

Ian Waldron, English Department Head,
North Toronto Collegiate,
Toronto, Ontario

To the Student

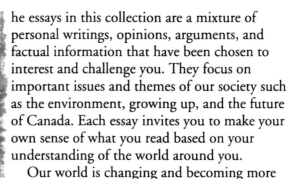

he essays in this collection are a mixture of personal writings, opinions, arguments, and factual information that have been chosen to interest and challenge you. They focus on important issues and themes of our society such as the environment, growing up, and the future of Canada. Each essay invites you to make your own sense of what you read based on your understanding of the world around you.

Our world is changing and becoming more complex daily. Only by thinking about information presented to us, and by considering the evidence presented to support opinions offered, do we come to feel more comfortable with our changing environment. The essays included in these pages provide you with a wide range of ideas to consider, discuss, and accept or reject. They have been written by people who share some common experiences with you. You won't always agree with them or agree with all that they say. Just because a viewpoint has been published doesn't mean that it's true. Make up your own mind about the opinions and information you read. Think it through. Talk about your responses with others.

The activities that follow the essays use the essays as starting points for your own explorations, research, discussion, and writing. As you listen to the responses of classmates, think about the evidence they use to support their ideas, and decide whether you agree with them. Just as you will not agree with all the ideas expressed by the writers of the essays, you will not always agree with arguments presented by your classmates. Listen to their ideas, and make up your own mind about the issues.

In your reading of these essays, and in the writing, speaking, and thinking you do in response to them, you increase your ability to interact successfully with your world. Enjoy the ideas and experiences presented in the essays and your own responses to them. Good luck and have fun.

Table of Contents

The Games of Our Lives

The Getting and Spending of Money

Acknowledgements

Growing Up

We all come from the past, and children ought to know what it was that went into their making, to know that life is a braided cord of humanity stretching up from time long gone, and it cannot be defined by the span of a single journey from diaper to shroud.

RUSSELL BAKER,
JOURNALIST

You grow up the day you have the first real laugh—at yourself.

ETHEL BARRYMORE,
ACTOR

Our youth have an insatiable desire for wealth; they have bad manners and atrocious customs regarding dressing and their hair and what garments or shoes they wear.

PLATO,
FOURTH CENTURY B.C. PHILOSOPHER

Growing up is the understanding that one's unique and incredible experience is what everyone shares.

DORIS LESSING,
WRITER

Adolescence: Challenges of the Teen Years

Nick Gallo

f you are now 12 years old, you are commonly considered a youngster. If you are 18, you are expected to behave as an adult. The six years in between are the critical years of your adolescence, the passage from childhood to adulthood.

So much happens during this transition—physically, emotionally, and socially. You see dramatic changes in your physical appearance, your inner feelings, and the social roles you are expected to fill. With so much to decide from among a sometimes bewildering array of life goals, lifestyles, and values, adolescence is a time of high excitement and opportunity.

There can also be many problems during this time period. The way of life in our society has become more complex and competitive, and this may be putting more pressure on you. Statistics on suicide, runaways, teen pregnancy, and drug abuse may suggest adolescence is a potential minefield.

Yet, another picture emerges when talking to researchers. Studies by Dr. Daniel Offer, chief of psychiatry at Michael Reese Hospital and Medical Center in Chicago, indicate 80 percent of teenagers handle the journey through adolescence with a minimum of difficulty.

"The vast majority of adolescents are normal, are relatively happy, and are hopeful about the future," says Offer. "They get along well with parents, teachers, and peers. That leaves 20 percent with problems, which is a large number, but the percentage is no higher than for any other age group."

By its nature, adolescence is a time of change; in fact, the Latin root of the word adolescence is "esso," which means "becoming."

Your chief task as an adolescent is "becoming"—developing the abilities, confidence, and desire to participate in the larger world. What are some of the obstacles? Which kinds of conflicts are normal—and which aren't? How do you get through the "storm and stress" of these years? The following information may be helpful.

Adolescence is often divided into three stages: early, middle, and late. Though every teenager is different, similar concerns crop up at each phase. In early adolescence, about ages 11 to 13 for girls and 12 to 14 for boys, the major issue usually is puberty—and how to adjust to natural physical and emotional changes. During your middle adolescent years, you are often searching for independence, which sometimes is at odds with rules laid down by parents. During late adolescence—age 17 and over—you commonly struggle to form your identity—the sense of who you are. It helps in the important choices you must make regarding education, work, and relationships.

At the age of 10 or 11 in girls and about 12 or 13 in boys, you reach puberty. At about this age, you can note the beginning of dramatic physical changes. Commonly, a growth spurt happens, lasting about three years. Boys may find the first signs of facial hair and hear their voices cracking. Girls have their first menstrual period. As a result of normal hormonal changes, many teenagers will also have some form of acne.

"The big question young adolescents have is 'what's normal?'" says Dr. James Farrow, director of the division of adolescent medicine at the University of Washington. "There's a wide range. They can develop several years ahead or behind one another and it's considered normal. Usually, the difference is temporary."

Because so many changes in appearance take place, you may be self-conscious about your body image. The way you think you look to others has a way of affecting how you feel about yourself. You may suddenly see yourself too fat, or too heavy in the wrong place, or too gawky, perhaps. Often this has little to do with reality. But a poor self-image can have negative consequences, stealing your confidence and ability to get along with others.

Your self-image also may be changing because your thinking and awareness at this time are also changing, evolving from the relatively straightforward demands of childhood to the ability to recognize complexities in situations. New behavior and reactions are being tried out, with the result that you may find yourself moody, inconsistent, and unsure of yourself, as was Anne Frank, who wrote in her *Diary of a Young Girl:* "A voice sobs within me. There you are, that's what's become of you: you're uncharitable, you look supercilious and peevish. People dislike you and all because you won't listen to the advice of your better half."

If you are a girl age 13 to 16 or a boy age 14 to 17, you are likely to have a different set of concerns, primarily those that involve independence. At this age, you are developing a personal code of beliefs and values, pulling away emotionally from your parents or other authority figures, to one degree or another. Some tension and friction is almost universal, since so many issues—such as dating, curfews, clothes budgets, using the car—involve decision-making. Outright rebelliousness, however, isn't as intense or widespread as the media suggest, according to studies. Most teenagers identify strongly with their parents' values.

There is no doubt, though, that the influence of parents is declining, in part because parents and teenage children typically spend so little time together. Studies of Chicago-area adolescents reveal that a father and teenager spend on the average just five minutes a day alone together, excluding meals, shopping, or watching television.

More time is being spent with peers—and being alone. Psychologist Mihaly Csikszentmihalyi (chk-sent-mi-ha-le) equipped high school students near Chicago with silent beepers that would go off randomly, signaling youths to write down what they were doing. The results showed teenagers spent more than *half* their time with friends and classmates, and more than a *quarter* of their time alone.

This separation from members of your family isn't necessarily bad. Learning about how to build outside relationships—how to be open, honest, and loyal with people—is part of growing up. Friends give feedback and support. Solitude also can be productive, providing calm, untroubled time to reflect.

There is, however, the risk of being drawn into a peer group that is out of control: one that drinks and uses drugs, for instance. This may not only be against the law, but it can have serious consequences. The leading killer of teenagers is motor vehicle accidents. Teenagers are involved in fatal crashes at a rate of more than double that of any other age group. Add drinking and the deadly mix of alcohol and motor vehicles doubles the rate of deaths yet again.

Serious, excessive behavior—not the occasional exuberant activity that almost everyone indulges in once in a while—is now being linked to depression. Some depression is normal. It's often a reaction to a loss of some sort, usually linked to specific events, and lasting no more than a few weeks.

More serious depression includes other symptoms, among them: low self-esteem, low motivation, less enjoyment of pleasurable activities, and changes in appetite and sleep. It's estimated that about 7 percent of adolescents have this more serious form of depression. They may reveal it in different ways, ranging from constant sleeping to anger to taking wild risks.

It's important not to ignore these signs. Adolescent suicide is an epidemic. The rate has increased 40 percent in the past decade. In most cases, teenagers contemplating suicide provide a clue. If you have such thoughts, *get help*. If you suspect a friend is considering suicide, notify someone who can help. You may save a friend's life.

Other troubled adolescents cry for help in less direct ways. Eating disorders are now a major problem among teenagers. Anorexia, marked by severe weight loss, is life-threatening. Bulimia, a disorder of secretive binge eating followed by self-induced vomiting, causes serious health problems. Stressful family relationships, as well as image-related pressures to look slim, are thought to contribute to the problems.

Some teenagers attempt to anesthetize their pain through drugs or alcohol. They may feel rotten about themselves; or there may be things about themselves they wish frantically they could change. Drugs seem to be the solution. Many reasons may surround why someone starts using drugs, but there's usually a common reason for continuing them: They become needed.

Drugs are habituating and sometimes addicting. They make people want to do them again and again.

What if you're in a situation where you have to decide whether to do drugs? Counselors suggest you make your decision ahead of time *before* that situation ever arises. Know the risks involved. This is a period of growth for you. If you experiment with any substance not needed to grow or maintain health, you're playing chemical Russian roulette.

Four years ago, the Search Institute of Minneapolis polled more than 8,000 young people and 10,000 adults and concluded that adolescents in a close family unit are the ones mostly likely to not use drugs, engage in sexual activity, or take part in other antisocial behavior. Good communication is at the heart of family closeness, reports Dorothy Williams of the Search Institute. "It takes very careful listening to have good communication," she says. "It takes mutual respect."

"Who am I?" asked Alice in *Alice in Wonderland*.

It's a common question you put to yourself as you reach the final years in high school and turn your attention to some major decisions involving education and work.

Spanning all of adolescence, and particularly intensified during the later teen years, is the main issue of identity. Some people go through what's popularly called an "identity crisis," which the famous psychoanalyst Erik Erikson called completely natural. In Erikson's view, adolescence is a stage of the life cycle when it's normal to ask: What do I want out of life? What things are important to me? What kind of person would I really like to be?

In countries like the United States, in which so many choices and paths exist, such a search for self can turn into a full-blown crisis. Fifty years ago, if you were a teenage boy growing up on a farm in rural America, you might have automatically turned to farming upon leaving school, inheriting your parents' goals and world view. Today, most teenagers face an immense range of options, which can make it more difficult to commit themselves to a course of action. Erikson believed it was a good thing to explore alternatives, contending it allowed adolescents a better chance to realize all they are capable of becoming.

Some researchers think adolescence is inherently stressful. Others attribute the turmoil surrounding many of today's teenagers to our society. More and more families today are headed by parents who are both working outside the home. More one-parent families exist. More family breakups occur. The divorce rate in our society has been estimated at 50 percent. While the effects of these developments on teenagers haven't been demonstrated yet, it's safe to say they will make the adolescent passage to adulthood at least more complicated.

Psychologist Csikszentmihalyi, co-author of *Being Adolescent*, believes what's missing for many teenagers is a sense that they have a purposeful role. He says adolescents need to do more activities that use their powers of attention and concentration. He calls these things "flow activities," and defines them as enjoyable activities that build your habits of discipline or skills, and that challenge you with increasingly complex goals. They engage your spirit and make you feel unique and special, and range from music to sports to being with your friends.

They are the kind of things that keep you moving through these years, growing—in many more ways than one—and going in the right direction as you chart this passage through adolescence.

Activities

1. With a partner, list the facts the essay provides about changes that occur during adolescence, problems faced by teens, and the positive side of adolescence. Be prepared to report to the class on the contents of your lists.

2. With a partner, identify what you would select as the most accurate and important point about adolescence that the author considers in the essay. Identify another point that you think is either inaccurate or unimportant. Be prepared to report your choices to the class for discussion.

3. With a partner, decide how many sections you think there are in this essay. For each section, provide a subheading to highlight its content. Be prepared to report to the class your choices and whether you prefer the essay with or without the subheadings.

4. Write a journal entry describing an important challenge that you face as an adolescent. It may be different from the ones identified in the essay.

5. In a group of three, prepare a questionnaire to survey attitudes of students in your school about the major problems of adolescence. After you have created the questions you want to ask, decide how many students you will include in your survey. Summarize the survey findings. Report the results in an article for the school newspaper.

What's Great About Teenagers

David Elkind

hy do you think we are so terrible?" a teenage girl asked me at a recent New England mall forum for teenagers and their parents. Then she continued, "You always blame us for everything. A few kids do something wrong at the skating rink or at the mall, and pretty soon you close the rink or don't let us in the mall after seven!" I had to admit that adults do sometimes behave as if all teenagers were a menace. I also reminded her that sometimes teenagers behave as if all adults were monsters.

Both positions are extreme. Generalizations about a particular age group, like generalizations about religious or ethnic groups, overlook the wide range of individual differences within any group.

So I won't try to describe what I believe is great about teenagers in general. Instead I will reminisce; as adults, the best way for us to appreciate what is great about today's teenagers is to recall those teenagers we knew and admired.

Russell and I became friends in junior high school in Detroit in the early forties. We both enjoyed books and often rode to the public library together on our bikes. Then the race riots began. Russell was one of the few blacks in our school. I was sure Russell would stay home. But he came to school every day. He never talked about the fear he must have experienced in walking past the National Guardsmen every day. Nor did he complain about those students who made insulting statements behind his back—or to his face. "Consider the source," he told me.

Soon after the riots ended, my family moved, and I lost touch with Russell. But I thought of him often, many years later, during all the battles of the civil rights movement. His willingness to challenge hatred is a testament to the courage of all young people who will not be humbled by prejudice and discrimination.

Although most of my high school friends were boys, I did have one female friend. Sandy was not really pretty, her nose was too long, and her figure had to be described as flat rather than curvy. But she had a great personality. Being with her was always fun. She never failed to have a project going: putting on a play, selling raffle tickets for charity, and falling in love were all wonderful adventures. Her enthusiasms were infectious, and she often coaxed me out of my shell to aid her in one of her new projects. To me, Sandy was what being young was all about.

Harold and I were never close friends. I remember him as something of a loner. We did have a math class together, and it gave me a chance to know him a little better. I remember that when we got our final exams back, he was angry and rebellious. Although he had gotten the right answers, he did not use the procedures the teacher had told us to use. He had come up with his own way of solving the problems and thought those that the teacher showed us were rather tedious and unimaginative. I suggested that he talk to the teacher, but he told me, "You do it their way, or else." Harold dropped out of school after the eleventh grade.

Some years later I was reminiscing with a high school friend I hadn't seen for years. "Do you remember Harold?" he asked. "I met him on a plane a couple of years ago. He's with a major computer company now, travels all over the world servicing mainframes, and is a real hot shot. They even sent him to college. He's making a bundle." Good for you, Harold, was my reaction.

Like these young people I admired, today's teenagers have qualities that make them unique and special. Before we parents generalize about teens, we need to acknowledge that they have as much to offer as the teens we once knew. Teenagers are people, warts and all, and that is what is so great about them.

Activities

1. For each teen described in the essay, identify the quality that the author admired in that person. List teen friends and acquaintances that you admire. For each one, summarize the quality or qualities the individual possesses that you admire.

2. With a partner, list features of the stereotypical teenager as viewed by some adults in our society. Discuss your responses to the following questions:
   - What is the basis for a stereotype?
   - In what ways are stereotypes useful?
   - In what ways are they unfair?

   Be prepared to report the results of your discussion to the rest of the class.

3. Write a short personality profile of an adolescent you know, highlighting characteristics of that individual.

4. In a group of four, prepare a presentation for the class in which you argue that the behaviour of teens today is better, worse, or about the same as ever.

Where the Child Is Father of the Man

Paul Fenn

hy are Indonesian kids so well behaved? Why are the poor in Indonesia essentially happy? Why are relatively rich Westerners essentially miserable?

Soon after I arrived in Indonesia, in May, 1989, I began to ask myself these questions. After a year of observing and travelling through most of Southeast Asia, I began to get some answers.

I think the first clues came to me on the island of Sulawesi (formerly Celebes), where I stayed for a couple of weeks with an Indonesian family.

By Indonesian standards, Robbie's family was pretty well off, but lived more or less like most Indonesians do. His wife was away in Jakarta for a month, so relatives and neighbors were helping out with the family's three-month-old baby.

After a few days there, I tried to pick Robbie's brains.

"How come your baby never cries?" I asked.

"We love her and play with her all the time," he replied.

"But in Canada, we do the same thing with our babies, and they do nothing but scream."

He shrugged his shoulders.

Over the next few days, I began to notice differences in approach. The baby was never left alone. If awake, she was played with and cuddled. If asleep, she was often in a cocoon-like sarong carried around someone's shoulder, or Grandma would lie next to her in the big bed and rub her stomach.

Everyone took a turn. Robbie's son, Hannes, would do his daily chores with the sarong full of baby on his back. Then Fatima from next door might take over for a while. Sometimes a neighbor would just walk in the house and take the baby across the street for an hour or so.

Baby was adored by all around her, yet never spent a long time with, or developed a dependence on, one particular person. As long as someone was there to do baby things with her, she was happy. Through that kind of upbringing, she was becoming more independent than the average Western baby, whose early childhood is spent with only one or two care-givers.

At 14, Hannes was already a good driver. The local policeman knew it, and that was good enough for him; they'd exchange waves while passing on the road. Hannes did most of the household shopping at the market. He was a kind and polite lad who did repairs on the family truck, knew local trees by their species names and the different uses for their timber—and he played a mean guitar. I never saw Robbie scold, let alone yell, at his son. They got along as two men of the same age would.

How can this be? I'd ask myself. The answer seems to be that kids want to do as their parents do. Robbie did the obvious: he let them.

Perhaps this is the substance of the solution to the horrible-teenager problem. When I was a useless teen, my granny used to say to me, "Paul, an idle mind is the devil's playground," inferring that my mind had gone unchallenged for so long that a sort of "rot" had set in. If such rot is permitted to fester through prolonged inactivity, self-esteem decays and a directionless haze clouds the psyche.

As soon as they are physically able, average Indonesian children are doing the day-to-day chores they'll have to do for the rest of their lives. Given that and the time spent playing, they have no time to become bored.

But most of us, as children, did not have to contribute significantly to the maintenance of our households. Youth had few responsibilities.

Probably the first thing I noticed about Southeast Asians in general was their playfulness. Women especially seem to possess a childlike, but not immature, desire to have fun. Could this be because they were brought up by their own brothers and sisters?

Everywhere I went in so-called undeveloped countries, I saw small children being raised by siblings often only 9 or 10 themselves. If children pass through their formative years reared primarily by other children, it seems natural they will retain many childlike qualities as adults. Even if there were influential adults in their early life, their "adult" influence would have been minimal because they too were likely raised by their brothers and sisters.

Material dearth, strong social and family bonds and values, the necessity of deriving a livelihood from the land and a devotion to religion are common denominators in the lives of most rural Indonesians. Westerners do not live within such a framework. We generally strive for more self-serving, less communally oriented ends.

Many have argued that cultures such as ours, which have time for leisure, become more "advanced" than cultures too busy surviving to think about ways to improve life or make it more interesting. However, having this time allows the "idle mind" syndrome to come into the picture. People with time on their hands have a chance to think about the little things in life that bother them. Friction exists within our families and communities because our culture encourages us to be vocal with one another about our feelings. Indonesia's does not. As a result, family and social life is typically harmonious.

Why do people have arguments and confrontations? Because one person perceives another to be infringing on his or her peace of mind or self-interest. Indonesians seldom disagree openly. If they are poor, they have few self-interests. For them it makes sense to co-operate with family members and the community at large, even if a sacrifice is involved. They depend on each other. Their peace of mind is derived from this inter-dependence and the fact that they live independently of large corporate or bureaucratic structures, a major cause of stress in our society.

It's impossible for us to exchange our ways for those of the Indonesians. Yet, if we promote within our children a responsibility for important aspects of the family's life, and we ourselves become less aggressive and selfish and perhaps more fatalistic, there are so many personal and social benefits that naturally accrue. Life simplifies, becomes less impersonal, more relaxed and just plain sweeter.

Activities

1. With a partner, list the reasons the author gives to explain why poor Indonesian children cry less than affluent Canadian children. Decide which reasons seem most valid to you. What other reasons can you think of? Be prepared to share your thoughts with the class.

2. With a partner, consider the effectiveness of the introductory and concluding paragraphs of this essay. Be prepared to tell the class the conclusions you reached and what criteria you used in making your decision.

3. Based on evidence from your own childhood, write a journal entry in which you agree or disagree with Paul Fenn's argument in this essay.

4. In a group of three, brainstorm at least four suggestions that you would make to improve the sense of belonging that teenagers have in our society. Compare your list with that of another group.

5. Do some research to find out about the needs of children in countries less fortunate than Canada. Based on your findings, make a poster encouraging people to contribute to an organization that supports needy children. Perhaps you could invite a representative from Care Canada, Foster Parents Plan of Canada, or UNICEF Canada to speak to the class.

Devils in Disguise: School-Yard Bullies Sabotage Their Own Futures

Carol Sevitt

welve-year-old Sarah was a born victim. A shy and retiring girl with learning problems and low self-esteem, she had few friends. When three girls at her public school in Halifax began following her after school, linking their arms and threatening to "get her," Sarah never hit back or replied. Unfortunately, her timid response fed right into the bullies' quest for power and set up a vicious cycle—the more passive she was, the more the bullies ganged up on her.

At one time or another in our lives, we've all come across school bullies. We've seen and felt their power—their endless taunting of weaker children, their cavalier lack of feelings and respect. For the victims, the humiliation of repeated attacks leaves a sense of powerlessness that may last a lifetime. As for the bully, new studies are sounding an alarm: evidence indicates that a lot of kids who bully grow up to be abusive adults. With the proliferation of teen gangs and the frightening increase in neighborhood violence, identifying and defusing the bully at an early age has become a new focus in many Canadian schools. In fact, the situation has prompted trustees at the Toronto Board of Education to launch a $25,000 project to find new ways of treating this old problem. This time, the emphasis is on dealing with the bully, rather than counselling the victim.

In an attempt to curb mounting violence, psychologists and educators around the world are placing bullies under a microscope to see what makes them tick. American studies have shown that when bullies grow up, they tend to become involved in violent crimes, abuse their spouses and work in dead-end jobs. Studies in Norway and Sweden conducted by Dan Olweus, a Swedish psychologist, revealed that about seven per cent of students in grades one to nine are bullies. In a six-year study of aggression in children, Dr. Richard Tremblay, a research psychologist at the University of Montreal, found that 19 per cent of Montreal boys and six per cent of the girls showed frequent aggression in kindergarten. About 40 per cent of these boys were still aggressive at the end of Grade 6.

Who are these bullies and why do they enjoy pushing other kids around? "Some bullies are wimps underneath, others are angry and mistreated and have little capacity to believe in relationships," says Dr. Margaret Whitfield, a Toronto child psychiatrist. Adds Bev Underhill, the principal of Lord Roberts Elementary School in Vancouver: "For some, it's the hitting and violence they've been subjected to at home. For others, it has to do with insecure feelings about themselves, a lack of confidence, or the inability to make friends."

Most bullies are boys, a fact that is not surprising considering the difference in socialization between boys and girls. Boys are encouraged to fight it out and be tough, while girls are encouraged to be more conciliatory. Other contributing factors are the higher incidence of school problems, learning disabilities and hyperactivity among boys, all of which are linked to bullying.

However, there are still plenty of girls who run roughshod over other children. They're not usually as physically aggressive as boys, often preferring to tease, ridicule or threaten their victims. In fact, this phenomenon provided the powerful theme of novelist Margaret Atwood's best-selling novel *Cat's Eye*, a haunting revelation of the terrors and betrayals of childhood. Painter Elaine Risley is in her late 40s but still menaced by the spectre of Cordelia, her best friend and the torment of her youth. Elaine's journey into the past evokes vivid images of the savage cruelty of children and the damaging repercussions—for the bully as well as the victim. Her final, compassionate understanding makes that clear: "There is the same shame, the sick feeling in my body, the same knowledge of my own wrongness, awkwardness, weakness; the same wish to be loved, the same loneliness; the same fear. But these are not my own emotions anymore. They are Cordelia's; as they always were."

Typically, bullies lack social skills, act impulsively and have a low frustration tolerance. They fly off the handle quickly, bloodying noses and pushing kids down before giving any thought to the consequences of such action.

They overpower other kids—especially kids who are physically smaller and weaker than they are. The passive, sensitive, insecure child is a typical victim. But bullies don't only pick on shy children—they pick on kids who are vulnerable in any number of ways. Kids who look, dress, act or speak differently often arouse the bully's aggressive instincts. Bullies have an uncanny ability to find a child's tender spot and zero in on it.

Although they actively seek power, many bullies end up without real power in later life. "Often bullies don't do well academically, drop out of school early and end up with dead-end, low-paying jobs," says Kenneth Goldberg, executive director of Earlscourt Child and Family Centre in Toronto. "Some of them end up in jail." Says Montreal's Richard Tremblay: "Most juvenile delinquents and adult criminals had conduct disorders as children, and about 30 to 40 per cent of children who have problems with aggression will retain these problems as adults." Professor Olweus's study of bullies determined that 40 per cent of bullies had at least three court convictions by the time they were 24.

Says Goldberg: "The tragedy of the bully is that because aggressive behavior can last into adulthood, today's bullies are at risk of being the wife and child abusers of tomorrow—and will set the stage for the next generation of bullies."

As a society, we must take a hard look at how we can help aggressive children at risk of becoming the teen gang members and criminals of the future. Research has shown that intervention can help bullies—and the earlier it is done, the more effective it is. An intervention program in Norwegian primary schools reduced the bully-victim problem by 50 per cent. The program included written information for teachers describing what they could do; a flyer for parents of victims, bullies and ordinary children; and a video about the lives of bullied children, which gave suggestions on how to handle problems.

The school must play a key role if bullying is to be eliminated. Removing a bully from the situation and sending him or her to the office does not help the bully learn how to get along better with peers. He or she must face real consequences for terrorist acts.

Teaching new attitudes takes time and practice, but much headway can be made by caring teachers. An effective method is involving children in role-playing in the classroom. Victims can be taught to say, "That hurts," or "That hurts my feelings," and bullies can begin to learn strategies for controlling their aggression. Bullies and victims are at opposite ends of a continuum, says David Cox, a therapist at the Atlantic Child Guidance Centre in Halifax. "Think of a scale with passive on the bottom, assertive in the middle and aggressive at the top. Bullies need to learn to move down the scale to assertive, and victims need to learn how to move up to assertive."

The staff working with aggressive children at Earlscourt use a technique called Stop Now and Plan (SNAP). When they feel trouble brewing, they snap their fingers. This is a signal for the children to stop what they're doing and count to 10, which gives them the opportunity to consider both options: "What will happen if I do bully?" "What will happen if I don't?"

But a school can only go so far, and parents need to shoulder an equal measure of responsibility. For starters, parents of bullies need to look to their own behavior. David Cox is adamant about abstaining from corporal punishment. "Spanking a child for being aggressive is the height of inconsistency," he says. Advises Kenneth Goldberg: "Consistently praise appropriate social behavior, and punish antisocial behavior. But don't over-punish, and avoid sarcasm. If you get a call from the school one day and they tell you your child has been bullying other children, listen to the teacher."

Experts say that parents should also monitor their children's TV viewing. Through depictions of murder, robbery and violence, bullies receive reinforcement for their aggressive actions. "Aggressive boys are attracted to aggressive shows," says Dr. Tremblay.

Parents can help their children—both bullies and victims—improve their social skills by encouraging them to join structured groups like the Boy Scouts and the Girl Guides, which provide opportunities for children to socialize in a more controlled setting than the school playground.

The ideal situation is that home and school work together. If teachers and parents both give the same message—that bullying is unacceptable and that the child will face specific consequences or lose certain privileges, there's a better chance of eliminating the problem. Firmness and consistency are critical. Home and school need to pull together to show the bully that aggression won't be tolerated and that the victim's pain is real.

Activities

1. With a partner,
   - identify where the author gives evidence that she has researched her topic,
   - list information the essay provides about
     - the causes of bullying behaviour in young people,
     - the characteristics of bullies and their victims,
     - what can be done to help young people control their aggressive behaviour.

2. Write a journal entry about aggressive behaviour you have observed or experienced in young people over the years. Comment on whether you think children are more aggressive today than they were when you were a child.

3. In a group of three, role play an incident that involves a bully, a victim, and a teacher, and that illustrates some of the points made in the essay. Perform it for the class and invite their comments.

4. Design a "Fight Back" brochure that explains to students what they can do if they are attacked by a bully.

5. Read a book or watch a film about a child or teen with a problem. Write a letter to the person with the problem as a friend he or she has turned to for help. Determine what kind of advice you will offer. Decide what approach in presenting the advice will be most helpful under the circumstances.

Reason to Live: A Special Report on Youth Suicide

Sally Armstrong

n hindsight, Joyce Whitney says her son had given all the signals: "Shawn wanted to sleep a lot, he was totally uninterested in anything around him. His mood changed from happy to angry, and that wasn't like Shawn. He was a bubbly, happy-go-lucky kid. Then, three days before his 18th birthday, he jumped off a five-storey building and died an hour and a half later in the hospital."

It's been two years now, and Joyce still blames herself for not realizing what was happening to Shawn. "Maybe if I'd known a little bit about suicide, I might have recognized the signs in my son. But I just started reading about it after it happened. I used to think those things don't happen to me, they happen to other people."

Youth suicide has increased an alarming 300 per cent in Canada since 1965, averaging 700 cases annually during the last three years [1984–1986], says the Canadian Task Force on Suicide in a report prepared for public release early this year [1987]. Suicide is the second leading cause of death for people aged 15 to 24, surpassed only by accidents; in some months or years, it's been the leading cause. And experts fear the actual numbers may be as much as 50 per cent higher, since some deaths reported as accidental may in fact be suicides. Furthermore, for every suicide, there are 100 attempts that fail.

The Suicide Information and Education Centre in Calgary, the only one of its kind in the world, reports a 78 per cent increase in requests for information in the past year [1986]. And perhaps even more telling are the results of a survey carried out last year [1986] in Dundas, Ont., a picturesque town of 20,000 in southwestern Ontario. A local public health team sent out 550 questionnaires to high school students asking them whether they would be interested in talking to a counsellor, and if so, what they would like to talk about. An astonishing 139 said yes, they'd like to talk to someone—about suicide.

Dr. Diane Solursh, director of the Canadian Task Force on Suicide, says, "The fact is, most people think about suicide. Most people fantasize about it. But most don't do it."

Suicide has long been a poorly understood subject shrouded by religious, legal and social taboos. You mustn't do it, and you mustn't talk about it. The fear and shame surrounding suicide are great, and they're at their height when a young person is the victim.

But now the closet door is opening. Suicide is no longer a criminal offence, and the church has softened its stand on the issue. Concerned parents, teachers and teens are learning some of the facts about suicide:

- People considering it give warning signals.
- It's not true that by talking about it you somehow cause it to happen.
- There is help available.
- It's preventable.

The task force, which began its work in 1980, has gathered new and much needed information about suicide in this country. Leading in the report's 40 recommendations is the need for education. Clearly, it's time we demystified suicide and started sharing information.

For Joyce Whitney, these efforts come too late. Joyce, who calls herself a survivor of suicide, says, "Our lives will never be whole again, but we're learning to cope, learning to live with it." Joyce and her husband separated about two months before Shawn died. Today, sitting with her son John in their Calgary living room, she painfully describes the feelings she's been struggling with. "We were very close, Shawn and I. I was more like a friend than a mom to him. We related to each other, so the question that lingers is, why didn't he turn to me? What was happening that I wasn't aware of? I could have helped. I wasn't in town when it happened; I was at my parents' home, his grandparents. Did he try reaching out for me in the end? He could have reached me by telephone. I've lived with that for a long time. There's so much guilt.

"I don't think people who commit suicide have any idea of the devastation they cause their families and friends. Suicide is a very selfish death. It's straight tunnel vision. Shawn may have thought that Mom, Dad, Johnny, Nana and Grandpa would miss him, but he couldn't have realized the total devastation, he couldn't have imagined what he has done to us."

John Whitney, now 19, wonders whether the family will ever get over it. "This is the second year, but it's still as hard as the first because there are memories of him and there are pictures around the house. We were around the same age, and we were just out of the fighting stage. We were buddies. All of a sudden, that was taken away. I was left with nothing, with an empty feeling. We were building something and it just ended without being finished. That's the hardest thing about the special times like Christmas, birthdays, when we'd laugh and do things together—it's just not there anymore. It's really hard to deal with."

John says he knows now that Shawn was reaching out for help at the end. "He called all his friends, he even called a friend in Florida, and he called me. He was really drunk. He didn't used to drink, but he'd been drinking a lot just before he died. You don't realize the signs until it's too late."

Another young man, now 25 years old, whom we'll call Tom, was luckier than Shawn. When he was 20, he too jumped off a five-storey building but miraculously survived: "When I woke up [in the hospital] after the fall, I felt a renewed hope in life. I thought that maybe I'd been given another chance.

"It hasn't been an easy struggle since the attempt, but I feel great now. I've completed a degree program at school; I'm on my way to a successful career. I have the type of friends I want and do the things I want to do. I enjoy life and feel that I make my own circumstances and that they don't control me. We have choices—I realize that now."

Tom says his problems go back to his childhood. "My upbringing wasn't that great. I was always unhappy. I thought that as soon as I could leave home and move far away and get a good job, things would be better. So I moved to a big city from a small town, but things got steadily worse. I thought there was no hope for a better future; things were just going to get worse. Then I became very serious about suicide. The only reason I'm here today is I couldn't get access to a higher building. There are a lot of high buildings in a city, but it's surprisingly hard to get on top of them unless you live there.

"It's disturbing even now to remember my hopelessness and my attitude that nothing could get better—when it was really just one of those tough spots in life."

His advice to young people with similar feelings: "Stick it out, stay busy, try to focus on something besides yourself, because things *will* get better, no matter how bad they are. Those rough spots will make you strong."

He also thinks people who are feeling suicidal should be able to talk about it. "It shouldn't be such a taboo subject; we need to increase the dialogue, not just for people who are about to commit suicide but for everyone." Tom agreed to tell his story because, he says, "I hope I can stop one person from doing what I did."

Tom's renewed faith in living is not unusual, says Cheryl Forchuk, a specialist in mental health nursing with the Hamilton/Wentworth public health department, who is based in Dundas, Ont. "I've worked with both adults and teenagers who are suicidal. Time and time again, when the crisis is past, that person says, 'Thank goodness I didn't go through with it.' Given the opportunity, I think most people will change their minds."

Forchuk is part of a team that runs a counselling drop-in centre for teens that was set up in response to the results of the Dundas questionnaire. The sign on the door reads: "Overwhelmed? Over 16? Over Pinder's—Wednesdays 4 to 6 p.m." (their offices are located over a store called Pinder's). She explains how the program began: "The school nurses were seeing an increasing number of teens who were attempting suicide, and hearing from troubled kids who didn't have access to counselling. We developed the questionnaire to see if they too perceived the need for an early intervention program." The results of the survey validated the nurses' perception, and in April 1986 the program began.

Although the staff is thinking of holding group sessions in the future, all counselling now is individual—although some kids bring a friend because it makes them feel better. "Most problems—breaking up with a boyfriend, getting along at home—are resolved in one visit," says Forchuk. "Our goal is to solve the problem in up to four sessions or refer the person to a place with facilities for long-term problem solving."

One of the difficulties with traditional treatment, Forchuk says, is that there's a waiting period, sometimes as long as two weeks. "When teens are in crisis, they want something right now. There are even disadvantages to the way Over Pinder's is set up, because it's only open one night a week. If a teen has a problem on Thursday, he or she has to wait almost a whole week to see us."

Centres like these across the country are hearing from more and more teenagers who need someone to talk to. One 17-year-old we'll call Katie told us her story at a drop-in centre near her home: "When I was little, my mom left home in the middle of the night and never came back. My dad didn't talk about her. I didn't even know if she was dead. Dad was living with his girlfriend. I didn't like her. Dad was drinking a lot, and it seemed that he cared more about his alcohol than he did about me. School was going badly—I was never any good at school. I'd just broken up with my boyfriend and was feeling really unwanted. All my life I felt really lonely. One night I decided I was too lonely, I didn't want to go through this pain anymore. I cut my wrist with a scalpel. When the blood started gushing out, I freaked. I stopped the bleeding with towels, and I cleaned up the mess. I never told anyone. I was too embarrassed to go to a counsellor."

Another girl we'll call Laurie, who's also 17, says, "When I was 13, I had a boyfriend my parents didn't approve of. We broke up one day, and later that night he came back to the house and raped me. My parents found out. They decided to press charges. I was afraid of what his friends would do to me. My parents said I was a tramp, that I wasn't good enough for anyone and I was incapable of caring about people. Everyone at school found out. They teased me all the time. I decided one night that I couldn't put up with it anymore. I emptied a bottle of Aspirins and lined them up along my dresser. I took them one at a time, wondering if things would ever get better, if my parents would ever change their opinion of me, whether or not I'd ever have any true friends. The Aspirins made me sick. Afterwards, I was ashamed of myself. I never told anyone until now.

"If I had a friend who was talking about suicide, I'd tell her that you can't give up trying, you can't quit. I'd tell her to give it time, and to convince herself that things will get better. I'd show her how they got better for me."

Fourteen-year-old Sandi (not her real name) didn't try to commit suicide. Like Joyce and John Whitney, she is a secondary victim of suicide—one of those left behind. "My brother shot himself to death last year. I was the one who found him. He'd left a note at his bedside that said, 'Sorry it happened this way. My life can't be worked out.'

"My brother and I were very close. I was half him, he was half me. Everyone thinks I'm OK because I smile, but I'm not; I've never been the same. I miss my brother all the time— especially because there's no one to talk to now. He was really a fun brother. I still talk to him sometimes—I write notes to him.

"If I had the chance to speak to other young people about suicide, I'd beg them never to do it. I'd say, look at all the pain and guilt you'll cause your family and your friends. I'd say, even though you're down, you never know what will become of you—maybe you'll be someone famous someday. I think my brother would have been a famous comedian."

All the young people we interviewed feel that distress phone lines and suicide prevention programs are key. The Teen Line in Calgary, a support line for teenagers, answered by teenagers, is the first one of its kind in Canada. Coordinator Katie Black says, "We work on the principle that a lot of kids want to talk about what's troubling them. A lot of them don't feel very comfortable with an older person, someone who might criticize them or look down their noses at them. Since our volunteers are teenagers too, they can really understand what the caller might be going through." Of about 265 calls a month, four per cent may be crisis calls. The volunteers have been trained to recognize the signs of suicide and to respond appropriately.

In Hamilton, the first suicide prevention program started in area schools in September 1986. Wayne Elgie, supervisory assistant in the adjustment services department at the Hamilton board of education, is also on the executive of the Hamilton and district council on suicide prevention. He says the council, which worked in conjunction with the board in the development of the suicide prevention curriculum, started in 1980 when a group of community care givers got together to discuss ways of preventing suicide. They had been counselling more and more people in their agencies about suicide and felt a collective community response would be a more effective means of prevention.

The role of the council is to educate the public about the warning signs of suicide, to promote research into the causes of suicide and to secure public support in its prevention. Elgie says, "We support the suicide prevention course offered by the school board 100 per cent. We feel suicide *is* preventable.

"It took a year to prepare the curriculum. Teachers go through 20 hours of in-service training prior to using it, and it's now [1987] being piloted at several high schools. Once the pilot program is complete, other school boards can have access to the program," he says.

It's a start. Communities across the country are waiting for information. People like Joyce Whitney are relieved that at last people are beginning to talk about suicide. "I really think people should bring it out in the open," she says. "It is affecting a lot of our young people. It's on the rise, and I think parents should be aware that it happens to good families, as well as bad families. I wish I'd known two years ago what I know now, and maybe Shawn would be here today. Maybe somewhere along the line, some child will be saved because of the articles being published today. It's what I hope for."

Activities

1. With a partner, evaluate the effectiveness of the introductory paragraph of this essay using the following questions:
   - Does it engage your interest?
   - Does it introduce the topic and thesis of the essay clearly?
   - Does it set the tone of the essay?
   Then evaluate the concluding paragraph using the following questions:
   - Does it introduce any new concepts?
   - Does it flow logically from the rest of the essay?
   - Does it summarize the points in the essay?

2. Develop your own list of reasons why so many teens commit suicide. Write a journal entry explaining what you think society could do to reduce the number of teen lives lost to suicide.

3. In a group of three, do some research on teen suicide. Using the school library or local resource centre, read articles on the topic. Present the most informative facts you discover in a report to the class.

4. There are a number of films available for rent on video that focus on teen suicide (such as *Ordinary People* and *The Dead Poet's Society*). Watch one of them and write a review of the film evaluating how effectively it explored the causes and effects of teen suicide.

5. Debate the following: Be it resolved that society puts too much pressure on teenagers today.

6. Invite a guidance counsellor to your class to describe the most common kinds of problems students experience and assistance programs that are available to them. Prepare questions in advance that you would like the guidance counsellor to address.

7. In a group of three, discuss ways your school encourages students to feel welcome. Consider additional things the school could do to help students feel accepted. Report your findings to the class.

A Touch of Humour

Lost Among the Girls

Rand Richards Cooper

hen I was 13, my parents sent me to a girls' school. Their intention was not to torture me. They just weren't happy with the local public and parochial schools, and the only alternative in our town was a small, private day school then accepting boys for the first time in its 100-year history.

My friends were skeptical. "That's that girls' school, right?" they said.

"No way!" I said. "Think I'm crazy, man?"

In September 1972, I entered the ninth grade with five other boys. We were pioneers; more boys were below us, in the lower school, but above us were solid walls of girls. Typically, there were only two or three of us in any given class—little islands of boys in a vast sea of tantalizing femininity.

Our heroes were the older girls, the seniors. We were their pets, the little brothers some of them didn't have. To us, they were goddesses. I recall a school ski trip to New Hampshire. The senior girls were sitting in the front of the chartered bus, laughing and talking and smoking cigarettes. At one point, they called a couple of us boys up to sit with them. One of the seniors, a veritable woman who was also the student council president, wanted to read aloud to us, she said, from a book that all men should know about.

It was overwhelming—a giddy feeling to be on such intimate terms with these young women. The flip side, however, was a serious shortage of male role models. Going to a girls' school means saying goodbye to rock bands and dances, to star athletes and pep rallies and cheerleaders. There was no car culture. No one saving to buy a motorcycle. No one who had experience with girls. No cool older guy whose progress down the hall you could watch with that mix of envy, worship and desperate hope for your own future that such figures can inspire.

Sometimes I longed for all of this. When a friend of mine was named prom king at his school, I was jealous. At our school, proms were considered laughably primitive. But each spring I would see guys in their rented tuxes, taking girlfriends out to dinner. I guess I sensed that even if a prom *was* silly and primitive, surely the mere fact of having negotiated one brought you one small step closer to a set of shared experiences which, eventually, would constitute manhood. And what tradition did we at our girls' school have to substitute for it? The head-mistress's tea?

As the person in charge of my manly training, my father faced these dilemmas with me. From the start, he had never completely trusted a school that had no football team. Not that he expected or ever wanted me to play football—but what kind of school wouldn't even have a team? What would a boy learn there about becoming a man? He himself had gone to a boys' school where he had lettered in three sports. For years, he had been telling me stories of his own high school heroes—star athletes who upon graduation had trooped off to Europe to fight Hitler. I, on the other hand, had 18-year-old girls reading Germaine Greer to me on the schoolbus. I'm sure my father wondered: was this a healthy setup for one's son? And if not, wasn't *he* responsible?

Because my father couldn't easily voice his doubts, he clamped down on them. But every now and then his uneasiness would surface. As a 10th grader, I started going out with an 11th-grade girl, and my father chafed at our driving around in *her* car, going to movies on *her* money. "Look," he finally said to me. "Doesn't it embarrass you to be squired around town like that?"

Not at all, I explained. She had a driver's license, I didn't; she had an allowance, I didn't.

My father's wallet was out in a flash. "Please," he said, handing me $10. "Take the girl to a movie."

Whatever I told the old man, however, I did have a sense of male pride. Put a normal American boy in a girls' school, and you can be sure he will twist himself into knots trying to prove he is a little man. Each Monday, we boys came to school armed with tales of wild weekends. Randy Conradi played football with unbelievably tough older guys who rode motorcycles and didn't care if they broke your arm when they tackled you. Howie Bruskin had an older brother with a van and an awesome sound system and a bunch of friends who cruised I-95 all Saturday night.

The point was not to give in wholly to the identity the school was peddling. Outside, on the front wall, the sign bearing the school's old name had not yet been changed. Each day we boys had to bear the bottomless humiliation of entering a building clearly labelled, in huge letters, A SCHOOL FOR GIRLS. In light of this, small acts of insolence were crucial. I recall an elderly local poet who gave a reading each spring at the school. Larry Jacobs dubbed him Rigor Mortis and then, during the reading, made horrible, deathlike grimaces at me from across the room. I knew it was rude and wrong to laugh, but boys weren't supposed to sit there and take poetry without *some* resistance. Didn't anyone recognize that?

A dozen years later, I returned to the school for a four-year stint as an English teacher. Instead of laughing at poetry, I was now trying to teach it.

Things had changed. Every other student was a boy. There was a headmaster instead of a headmistress. The alma mater no longer sang the praises of sisters and daughters. Sports teams were thriving; there was a case of gleaming trophies and a roomy new gym. Student rock groups with names like Question Authority blasted the airwaves at dances. There was even a prom.

One day after school, on an impulse, I took one of my students—a boy—out to the front of the building, to the wall with the sign. The words had long ago been changed, but you could still see the holes where the old letters had been affixed. Look closely at those holes, I said. What do you see?

I waited while he squinted at the wall. Finally he gave up.

"It says 'A School For Girls,'" I said. "Can you believe that? When I went here this place was called a school for girls."

"Wow, Mr. Cooper," he said, politely. "That's pretty wild." Then, excusing himself, he went back into the school, where his band was practicing.

I stood there, alone, looking up at the dots and wondering just what it was I wanted the boy to understand. I knew it had something to do with being a man. It also had something to do with being outnumbered and overwhelmed. The experience of being in a minority does not come easily to a white male in America. But for a boy in a girls' school it is a burning reality.

Lost among the women, he knows both the sting of resentment and the mixed blessings of tokenism. He is granted a special status that brings special affection—but even this reminds him how excluded and marginal he really is. So he sticks together with the few of his own, and experiences the paradox of a group affiliation, which both hinders and enriches identity.

When I close my eyes and recall how those letters looked, I can still feel a tiny wave of the shame that rolled through my stomach each time I passed them. Why is it that a boy regards being called a girl with such deep terror? Do we men teach them this? Do we still carry this fear ourselves? Or have we made progress—have we indeed become the sensitive individuals the culture sporadically heralds?

I'm not so optimistic—not for myself, at least. My student looked up at the sign and said, in effect, what's in a name? And far from being glad for him, I was annoyed. That wasn't just any name: that sign said a school for *girls*. I wanted him to be a man and feel the shame.

Activities

1. With a partner, identify how each of the following felt about the narrator being one of six boys in the ninth grade:
   - the young man's father
   - the young man while at school
   - the young man today
   - the older girls at the school
   - the narrator's student

2. The essay identifies purposes schools have beyond being facilities for students to acquire academic knowledge and skills. With a partner, list these purposes, ordering them from the most to the least important. Add to your list based on your own experience. Using the list you develop, write an essay on the most important goals of the high school years.

3. With a partner of the same sex, discuss your opinions about the advantages and disadvantages of being in a situation similar to the one described in the essay. Compare your lists with those of a partner of the opposite sex. Report any differences you observe between the way males and females view the situation.

4. Write a journal entry explaining whether you would or would not want to be part of a minority group within a school.

5. Debate the following: Be it resolved that the generation of students in high school today provides hope for a kinder, saner society.

6. In a group of three, role play a humorous situation that could arise from the circumstances described in this essay.

A Place to Stand On

Margaret Laurence

"The creative writer perceives his world once and for all in childhood and adolescence, and his whole career is an effort to illustrate his private world in terms of the great public world we all share."
Graham Greene, Collected Essays

 believe that Graham Greene is right in this statement. It does not mean that the individual does not change after adolescence. On the contrary, it underlines the necessity for change. For the writer, one way of discovering oneself, of changing from the patterns of childhood and adolescence to those of adulthood, is through the explorations inherent in the writing itself. In the case of a great many writers, this exploration at some point— and perhaps at all points—involves an attempt to understand one's background and one's past, sometimes even a more distant past which one has not personally experienced.

This sort of exploration can be clearly seen in the works of contemporary African writers, many of whom re-create their people's past in novels and plays in order to recover a sense of themselves, an identity and a feeling of value from which they were separated by two or three generations of colonialism and missionizing. They have found it necessary, in other words, to come to terms with their ancestors and their gods in order to be able to accept the past and be at peace with the dead, without being stifled or threatened by that past.

Oddly enough, it was only several years ago, when I began doing some research into contemporary Nigerian writing and its background, that I began to see how much my own writing had followed the same pattern—the attempt to assimilate the past, partly in order to be freed from it, partly in order to try to understand myself and perhaps others of my generation, through seeing where we had come from.

I was fortunate in going to Africa when I did—in my early twenties—because for some years I was so fascinated by the African scene that I was prevented from writing an auto-biographical first novel. I don't say there is anything wrong in autobiographical novels, but it would not have been the right thing for me—my view of the prairie town from which I had come was still too prejudiced and distorted by closeness. I had to get farther away from it before I could begin to see it. Also, as it turned out ultimately, the kind of novel which I can best handle is one in which the fictional characters are very definitely *themselves*, not me, the kind of novel in which I can feel a deep sense of connection with the main character without a total identification which for me would prevent a necessary distancing.

I always knew that one day I would have to stop writing about Africa and go back to my own people, my own place of belonging, but when I began to do this, I was extremely nervous about the outcome. I did not consciously choose any particular time in history, or any particular characters. The reverse seemed to be true. The character of Hagar in *The Stone Angel* seemed almost to choose me. Later, though, I recognized that in some way not at all consciously understood by me at the time I had had to begin approaching my background and my past through my grandparents' generation, the generation of pioneers of Scots-Presbyterian origin, who had been among the first to people the town I called Manawaka. This was where my own roots began. Other past generations of my father's family had lived in Scotland, but for me, my people's real past—my own real past—was not connected except distantly with Scotland; indeed, this was true for Hagar as well, for she was born in Manawaka.

The name Manawaka is an invented one, but it had been in my mind since I was about seventeen or eighteen, when I first began to think about writing something set in a prairie town. Manawaka is not my hometown of Neepawa—it has elements of Neepawa, especially in some of the descriptions of places, such as the cemetery on the hill or the Wachakwa valley through which ran the small brown river which was the river of my child-hood. In almost every way, however, Manawaka is not so much any one prairie town as an amalgam of many prairie towns. Most of all, I like to think, it is simply itself, a town of the mind, my own private world, as Graham Greene says, which one hopes will ultimately relate to the outer world which we all share.

When one thinks of the influence of a place on one's writing, two aspects come to mind. First, the physical presence of the place itself—its geography, its appearance. Second, the people. For me, the second aspect of environment is the most important, although in everything I have written which is set in Canada, whether or not actually set in Manitoba, somewhere some of my memories of the physical appearance of the prairies come in. I had, as a child and as an adolescent, ambiguous feelings about the prairies. I still have them, although they no longer bother me. I wanted then to get out of the small town and go far away, and yet I felt the protectiveness of that atmosphere, too. I felt the loneliness and the isolation of the land itself, and yet I always considered southern Manitoba to be very beautiful, and I still do. I doubt if I will ever live there again, but those poplar bluffs and the blackness of that soil and the way in which the sky is open from one side of the horizon to the other—these are things I will carry inside my skull for as long as I live, with the vividness of recall that only our first home can have for us.

Nevertheless, the people were more important than the place. Hagar in *The Stone Angel* was not drawn from life, but she incorporates many of the qualities of my grandparents' generation. Her speech is their speech, and her gods their gods. I think I never recognized until I wrote that novel just how mixed my own feelings were towards that whole generation of pioneers—how difficult they were to live with, how authoritarian, how unbending, how afraid to show love, many of them, and how willing to show anger. And yet, they had inhabited a wilderness and made it fruitful. They were, in the end, great survivors, and for that I love and value them.

The final exploration of this aspect of my background came when I wrote—over the past six or seven years—*A Bird in the House*, a number of short stories set in Manawaka and based upon my childhood and my childhood family, the only semi-autobiographical fiction I have ever written. I did not realize until I had finished the final story in the series how much all these stories are dominated by the figure of my maternal grandfather, who came of Irish Protestant stock. Perhaps it was through writing these stories that I finally came to see my grandfather not only as the repressive authoritarian figure from my childhood, but also as a boy who had to leave school in Ontario when he was about twelve, after his father's death, and who as a young man went to Manitoba by sternwheeler and walked the fifty miles [80 km] from Winnipeg to Portage la Prairie, where he settled for some years before moving to Neepawa. He was a very hard man in many ways, but he had had a very hard life. I don't think I knew any of this, really knew it, until I had finished those stories. I don't think I ever knew, either, until that moment how much I owed to him. One sentence, near the end of the final story, may show what I mean. "I had feared and fought the old man, yet he proclaimed himself in my veins."

My writing, then, has been my own attempt to come to terms with the past. I see this process as the gradual one of freeing oneself from the stultifying aspect of the past, while at the same time beginning to see its true value—which, in the case of my own people (by which I mean the total community, not just my particular family), was a determination to survive against whatever odds.

The theme of survival—not just physical survival, but the preservation of some human dignity and in the end some human warmth and ability to reach out and touch others—this is, I have come to think, an almost inevitable theme for a writer such as I, who came from a Scots-Irish background of stern values and hard work and puritanism, and who grew up during the drought and depression of the thirties and then the war.

This theme runs through two of my novels other than *The Stone Angel* (in which it is, of course, the dominant theme). In *A Jest of God* and *The Fire-Dwellers*, both Rachel and Stacey are in their very different ways threatened by the past and by the various inadequacies each feels in herself. In the end, and again in their very different ways and out of their very different dilemmas, each finds within herself an ability to survive—not just to go on living, but to change and to move into new are as of life. Neither book is optimistic. Optimism in this world seems impossible to me. But in each novel there is some hope, and that is a different thing entirely.

If Graham Greene is right—as I think he is—in his belief that a writer's career is "an effort to illustrate his private world in terms of the great public world we all share," then I think it is understandable that so much of my writing relates to the kind of prairie town in which I was born and in which I first began to be aware of myself. Writing, for me, has to be set firmly in some soil, some place, some outer and inner territory which might be described in anthropological terms as "cultural background." But I do not believe that this kind of writing needs therefore to be parochial. If Hagar in *The Stone Angel* has any meaning, it is the same as that of an old woman anywhere, having to deal with the reality of dying. On the other hand, she is not an old woman anywhere. She is very much a person who belongs in the same kind of prairie Scots-Presbyterian background as I do, and it was, of course, people like Hagar who created that background, with all its flaws and its strengths. In a poem entitled "Roblin Mills, Circa 1842," Al Purdy said:

> They had their being once
> and left a place to stand on

They did indeed, and this is the place we are standing on, for better and for worse.

I remember saying once, three or four years ago, that I felt I had written myself out of that prairie town. I know better now. My future writing may not be set in that town—and indeed, my novel, *The Fire-Dwellers*, was set in Vancouver. I may not always write fiction set in Canada. But somewhere, perhaps in the memories of some characters, Manawaka will probably always be there, simply because whatever I am was shaped and formed in that sort of place, and my way of seeing, however much it may have changed over the years, remains in some enduring way that of a small-town prairie person.

Activities

1. With a partner, list at least five ways Margaret Laurence says her writing career was influenced by the world of her childhood and adolescence.

2. In a journal entry, describe places and people in your early life that you feel have had a lasting positive or negative influence on you.

3. Based on this essay, write a journal entry describing the kind of person Margaret Laurence was. You might indicate whether or not you think you would have gotten along with her.

4. With a partner, brainstorm ways in which people's lives are influenced by their childhood experiences. You might consider occupations, fears, and special interests or hobbies.

5. a) Do some research on the childhood life of Margaret Laurence and prepare a report to read to the class
   OR
   b) read one of Margaret Laurence's short stories and report on it to the class. See if you can find evidence of her "small-town prairie person" beginnings.

The Thinking Tree

Greg Clary

We spent a lot of summer days up in that tree, my friend Danny Grove and I. It's been twenty-five years since then, and though the summers on Maple Island now seem to run together, I can still remember the exhilaration of sitting hidden in the leafy branches of the tree we used to call the Thinking Tree.

As trees go, that old poplar wasn't remarkable at all. Other trees were taller or better for climbing, but none offered the same perspective on the world below. When Danny and I climbed up high in the Thinking Tree, somehow we always seemed to figure things out—hard questions and easy ones alike.

It didn't start out like that. We were just smart enough to realize a good thing when we found it—and to keep it a secret from the other kids, who might break the spell.

The two of us didn't have truly weighty problems to wrestle with then, but there were plenty of little boy questions that could not be answered without some study, and we knew where to go for that.

Sometimes we would try to figure out why we weren't allowed to swim out to the raft like the bigger kids. Other times we dreamed about the day we could finally go to work, like our dads. Often we plotted where to go next on our broom-handle horses, riding the range in search of bad guys to bring to justice.

Almost every day Danny and I would sit and conjure up a new superhero we'd like to be (and plan to corner Dan's grandma to sew the newest emblems on our capes). We spent a lot of time inventing superstrengths and superweaknesses, to make sure our titan battles would not be lopsided.

The only predators in our island paradise were our two older brothers—ogres who laughed out loud as they pulled our underwear up to our ears or pressed their knuckles into our heads. We were not really scared of our brothers—their torture was an accepted way of life. But for some reason our superpowers always seemed to disappear when we ran into them, so we learned to wriggle and run fast and use our wits to elude their grasp.

The tree was our sanctuary. We would race to it from wherever we were, a starter's gun going off silently in our heads, each boy for himself. It was never a real contest between us, though, because as often as not the loser would still get the best seat in the tree. That's the kind of friends we were.

There was one branch on the tree that split to form a natural seat complete with a back made from a smaller branch. It was the width of a man's fist, curving as if someone had sat there the whole time it grew.

Neither one of us spent much time wondering how the seat came to be; all we knew was that leaning back in that spot we came up with the best ideas. There was no arguing with success. We thought the tree had magical powers and had no reason to believe otherwise. After all, the biggest thing about us in those days was our imaginations.

Lately I find myself wondering where the sanctuary of that tree has gone. I can no longer run away to my favorite limb when I need answers. So much has changed in the intervening years—even swimming and running are now done more out of obligation than exuberance. Chasing after the bad guys has become a high-stakes game that is best left to people besides myself. And Danny Grove and I live a time zone apart and never seem to talk long enough to solve all our problems.

Recently I went back to Maple Island and visited the Thinking Tree to see if I had left the magic there. As I reached for the first branch, it still bent a little as it had long ago, but the other familiar feelings had vanished. I wanted to blame the changes on the tree, but as I climbed I realized the solace it symbolized hadn't disappeared altogether, it had just moved on. Now it was up to me to look for it again, to find a bower of solitude within my own busy life.

Afterwards, as I sat on the ground thinking about nothing in particular, I watched a group of kids walk by. I could have sworn I saw one small boy stare knowingly up into the leaves.

Activities

1. With a partner,
    - list three statements the author makes that reveal what sort of person he is,
    - list places you might seek as "bowers of solitude" within your own busy lives.

    Be prepared to share your lists with the rest of the class.

2. With a partner, write a dialogue between the author and his friend Danny Grove that uses a similar tone and similar facts to the ones revealed in this essay. Be prepared to identify the tone and explain how the details of your dialogue help to create it.

3. As the editor of a local paper, you are considering this essay for publication. You decide to publish it, but find that it is just a bit too long for the space available. You will need to cut one paragraph. Select the paragraph you would cut that would least alter the essay's meaning. Be prepared to defend your choice.

4. Select two descriptive sections from the essay that you like best and explain what you liked about them.

5. In your journal, write about
    - a memory of your early life that stands out vividly,
    - a special place in your life.

End of Unit Activities

1. Write a letter of advice to a teenage friend in which you clearly identify the problem and the advice you are offering. Follow correct letter format.

2. For a one week period, make a collection of all the news articles you find that focus on children and teens. Write your thoughts about the impression this collection of stories gives about the lives of children and teens in Canada today.

3. Write a description of a typical week in the life of a Canadian teenager that you could send to a pen pal in another country.

4. Research and read the 1989 United Nations Convention document on the Rights of the Child. Write a short essay on one of the articles in the document that particularly interests you.

5. Debate one of the following resolutions. Research may be necessary.
   - Be it resolved that a high school education should be required for anyone under twenty wishing to get a driver's licence.
   - Be it resolved that youth is wasted on the young.
   - Be it resolved that adolescence is the best (or worst) of times in a person's life.
   - Be it resolved that a Japanese education is superior to a Canadian education.

6. Write an essay on one of the following topics. Research may be necessary.
   - the ideal length of life
   - peer pressure
   - childhood and adolescence are the best or worst of times
   - the difference between life for a teenager today and life for a teenager fifty years ago
   - the early years of a great Canadian

Our Fellow Creatures

All things bright and beautiful,
All creatures great and small,
All things wise and wonderful,
The Lord God made them all.

CECIL FRANCES ALEXANDER,
POET

Animals are such agreeable friends—they
ask no questions, they pass no criticisms.

GEORGE ELIOT,
NOVELIST

I think I could turn and live with animals,
they're so placid and self-contain'd,
I stand and look at them long and long.

WALT WHITMAN,
POET

Physiological experiment on animals is
justified for real investigation, but not for mere
damnable and detestable curiosity.

CHARLES DARWIN,
NATURALIST

Playing Dice With Megadeath

Jared Diamond

n May 21, 1534, the French explorer Jacques Cartier stopped at Funk Island, off the coast of Newfoundland, so that his crew could feed on the meat of the great auk, a large, flightless seabird they could easily capture. After taking their fill, Cartier and his crew went on to explore the St. Lawrence River, and the great auks on Funk Island were safe for the next two and a half centuries—until feather collectors, searching out stuffing for pillows and mattresses, paid the birds a visit in 1785. Over the next half century the demand for the birds' feathers brought a steady stream of collection parties; by 1841 the great auks of Funk Island were gone completely.

So were most of their kin throughout the world. The last great auk on the Orkney Islands, north of Scotland, was killed in 1812; the last on St. Kilda, west of Scotland, in 1821; the last on the Faroe Islands, between Scotland and Iceland, in 1828. Six years later someone bagged the last great auk in Ireland. Finally, on June 3, 1844, two fishermen, Jón Brandsson and Siguror Islefsson, killed the world's last breeding pair at Eldey Rock, an island off the southern coast of Iceland; they also smashed the birds' single egg.

Although it is one of the most famous examples of extinction, the great auk is clearly not the only animal to disappear in modern times. The great auk is not even the only *bird* to become extinct. In North America alone we no longer have any living examples of the spectacled cormorant, the Labrador duck, the Carolina parakeet, and the passenger pigeon. Bachman's warbler, a resident of the swampy woods of the South, may be next on the list; it may already be gone—the most recent definite sighting was in 1977.

Everywhere humans have gone, they have wiped out whole species of birds, mammals, reptiles, fish, and other forms of life. Indeed, we continue to do so on every continent and island we inhabit, except now we act with a technology and a capacity for destruction far greater than that of our forebears. Many of us—scientist and nonscientist alike—find our increased threat to other species alarming. We fear that we have set in motion a wave of extinction that will ultimately undermine the quality, and perhaps even the possibility, of human life.

Not everyone, however, agrees that the risk of mass extinction is real, nor for that matter that it would do us much harm if it in fact occurred. One of the most frequently cited estimates in the debate, for example, is that humans have caused one percent of all bird species to become extinct within the past few centuries. Yet it's easy to imagine that most birds are superfluous as far as human needs are concerned and that we could safely lose, say, ten times more. We might even believe the same of other endangered species, from gray wolves to blue whales—it would be a pity to lose them, but life would go on.

What is the truth of our situation? Is the mass extinction crisis a hysterical fantasy, a real risk for the future, or a proven event that's already well under way? To answer those questions, we need to step back a bit and examine how the numbers bandied about by both sides in the debate are really arrived at. Then we need to know whether the pace of extinctions is rising or falling; we have to compare modern records with evidence dug up from the past. Finally, we need to ask what difference the loss of species makes. If more do become extinct, so what? How much do chickadees contribute to our gross national product anyway?

Birds keep popping up in the estimates for good reason: they are easy to see and identify, and hordes of bird-watchers keep track of them. As a result, we know more about birds than about any other group of animals, and so they provide a measure of the current destruction.

We know that approximately 9,000 species of birds exist today. Since only one or two new species are being discovered each year, we can safely say that virtually all living birds have been identified. According to the International Council for Bird

Preservation (the world's leading agency concerned with the status of birds), 108 species, a little more than one percent of the total, have become extinct in modern times—that is, since 1600, a date that conveniently marks the beginning of scientific classification.

Is this a fair measure of the rate of extinction? The council's list is intentionally conservative: a bird is registered as extinct only after it has been unsuccessfully searched for in all areas where it might conceivably turn up, and after it has not been found for many years. So there is little doubt about the true status of a bird listed as extinct. Can we be equally certain that all those bird species that have not fulfilled the council's rigorous criteria for extinction still exist? For North American and European birds the answer is yes. The presence of hundreds of thousands of fanatic bird-watchers virtually guarantees that no bird on these continents could drift into extinction unnoticed. In many cases researchers have watched a population dwindle to a few individuals and then followed the fates of those last survivors.

For example, the most recent casualty in the United States is the sub-species known as the dusky seaside sparrow, which lived in marshes near Titusville, Florida. As the marshes were destroyed, the sparrows' population shrank. Wildlife agents put identification bands on the remaining sparrows so that they could recognize each individual. When only six remained, they were brought into captivity; unfortunately, they were all males. On June 16, 1987, the dusky seaside sparrow became extinct— with witnesses.

But most tropical countries, where the overwhelming majority of species live, have few, if any, bird-watchers. The fate of many tropical birds is unknown, because no one has seen them or specifically looked for them since they were discovered years ago. Many other species were described from single specimens collected by nineteenth-century explorers who gave only vague indications of the site—such as "South America." We know nothing about the songs, behavior, and habitats of such birds, and even the most dedicated bird-watchers would be hard-pressed to identify one of those birds if they glimpsed or heard it.

Many tropical species therefore cannot be classified as either "definitely extinct" or "definitely in existence," but just as "of unknown status." It becomes a matter of chance which of these species happens to attract the attention of some ornithologist, be searched for, and then possibly be listed as extinct.

Here's an example: The Solomon Islands are one of my favorite birding areas in the tropical Pacific. The International Council for Bird Preservation lists one Solomon bird species, Meek's crowned pigeon, as extinct. But when I tabulated recent observations of all 164 known Solomon birds, I noticed that 12 had not been encountered since 1953. At least some of those 12 species are almost surely extinct. Some should have been sighted if they still exist because they were formerly abundant and conspicuous. Some, Solomon Islanders told me, have been exterminated by cats—a predator that missionaries and traders introduced.

Twelve species possibly extinct out of 164 still may not sound like much to worry about—a bit over 7 percent. However, the Solomons are in better shape environmentally than most of the remaining tropical world. These islands have few people, little economic development, and much natural forest. More typical of the tropics is Malaysia, which has had most of its lowland forest cut down.

And in Malaysia we have good records for a group of animals other than birds. Before the advent of massive logging in Malaysia, biological explorers identified 266 fish species in the region's forest rivers. A recent four-year search turned up only 122 of those 266, fewer than half. The other 144 must be extinct, rare, or very local. And they reached that status before anyone noticed.

Malaysia is typical of the tropics in the pressure it faces from humans. Fish are typical of tropical species other than birds in that they attract only patchy scientific attention. The estimate that Malaysia has already lost, or nearly lost, half its freshwater fish is therefore a reasonable ballpark figure for the status of animals and plants in much of the rest of the tropics. Even this estimate, however, applies only to species we have already discovered and described. What about the ones we have never seen or named? Are they too becoming extinct?

Fewer than 2 million plant and animal species have been described, but sampling procedures suggest that the actual number of the world's species may be at least 30 million. Most of them live in rain forests that biologists are just beginning to explore; over 1,500 beetle species, for example, have been found in a single species of tree in Panama.

Humans are now bearing down on this vast, unknown majority of species, and here and there we can glimpse the results. When botanist Alwyn Gentry, for example, surveyed an isolated ridge in Ecuador called Centinela, he found 38 new plant species, many of them strikingly beautiful, confined to that one spot. Shortly afterward the ridge was logged, and those plants were exterminated. On Grand Cayman Island in the Caribbean, zoologist Fred Thompson discovered two new species of land snails confined to a forest on a limestone ridge. When that ridge was cleared a few years later for a housing development, the snails disappeared.

The accident of Gentry and Thompson visiting those ridges before rather than after they were cleared means that we have names for the now-extinct species that lived there. But biologists don't first survey most tropical areas that are being developed. Humans must have exterminated plants and animals on innumerable other tropical ridges before anyone had a chance to discover them.

In short, then, published lists of species known to be extinct must be gross underestimates of the actual numbers. There is a systematic tendency to underestimate extinctions even among birds, which we know best. For many other forms of life the unknown species—and unknown extinctions—must far outnumber the known.

So far we have counted only species exterminated in modern times, that is, since 1600. But were there no exterminations before 1600, throughout the preceding several million years of human history? To find out if the slaughter is gaining momentum, we need to follow the swath we have cut through the past.

Until 50,000 years ago, when humans first reached Australia and New Guinea, we were confined to Africa plus the warmer areas of Europe and Asia. We reached Siberia 20,000 years ago,

North and South America 11,000 years ago, and most of the world's remote oceanic islands only within the past 4,000 years. Over this same period we were dramatically improving our hunting skills and our tools, and developing the technology of agriculture. Also, while expanding over the globe, we were increasing in numbers, from perhaps a few million 50,000 years ago to half a billion in 1600.

Paleontologists have studied many of the areas humans have reached within the past 50,000 years. In every one, human arrival coincided with massive extinctions. After people arrived in Australia, that continent lost its giant kangaroos and other giant marsupials. Around the time humans reached North America, that continent lost its lions, cheetahs, horses, mammoths, mastodons, giant ground sloths, and several dozen other large mammals. In all, counting by genus, 73 percent of North American large mammals became extinct near the time of human arrival. In South America it was 80 percent, and in Australia 86 percent.

We know that people hunted many of these animals. And in areas where meaty mammals were not abundant, people killed other prey. For example, paleontologists have found remains of recently extinct bird species on almost every oceanic island they have explored. New Zealand lost its giant flightless moas when the Polynesians arrived, and Hawaii lost its flightless geese and dozens of smaller birds. Extrapolation to islands not yet explored by paleontologists suggests that 2,000 bird species—one-fifth of all the birds that existed a few thousand years ago—fell victim to prehistoric exterminations. That doesn't count birds that may have disappeared on the continents.

Ever since researchers became aware of these prehistoric extinctions, they've debated whether people were the cause or just happened to arrive while animals were succumbing to climatic changes. But in the case of Polynesia, at least, there is now no reasonable doubt. Extinctions there not only coincided with human arrival but also with a time when climate was stable. Humans did turn up the heat, though—abandoned Polynesian ovens contain the bones of thousands of roasted moas.

To me the evidence seems overwhelming that humans played a role in the earlier extinctions also, especially in Australia and the Americas. In each part of the world in question, a wave of extinction swept over the land after the arrival of humans but didn't appear simultaneously in other areas undergoing similar climatic swings. If climatic changes at the end of the most recent ice age finished off America's big beasts, it's curious that those animals, having survived the previous 22 ice ages, chose to drop dead at the end of the twenty-third, just when human hunters sauntered by.

Moreover, it wasn't just in these newly occupied territories that large animals disappeared. In areas long occupied by humans, a new round of extinctions started 20,000 years ago: Eurasia lost its woolly rhinos, mammoths, and giant deer (the "Irish elk"). At the same time, Africa lost its giant buffalo, giant hartebeests, and giant horses. Like their cousins on the other continents, these big beasts may have been done in by pre-historic humans who hunted them with newer, better weapons.

Evidently, our species has a knack for exterminating others, and we're becoming better killers all the time. The key question for our children, though, is whether the crest of the extinction wave has already passed or whether the worst is still to come.

There are a couple of ways to approach this question. One is simply to assume that the number of tomorrow's extinct species will bear close resemblance to the number of today's endangered ones. Among birds an estimated 1,666 species—18 percent of the total—are now either endangered or at imminent risk of extinction. But this figure is an underestimate for the same reason that one percent is too low an estimate for birds we have already driven to extinction. Both numbers are based only on species whose status caught someone's attention, not on a reappraisal of all birds. The real number of species at risk must be higher.

The alternative approach to prediction is not to look at other species but rather to look at ourselves. Our destruction of others has kept pace with our population and technology, and it is fair to reason that this will continue until our population and technology reach a plateau. But neither shows signs of leveling off. Our population grew from half a billion in 1600 to more than 5 billion now, and it is still growing at close to 2 percent per year. And every day brings new technological advances by which we are changing Earth and its denizens.

If we are to predict the extent of our future devastation, then we must take notice of the mechanisms by which we cause extinction. Of the four leading ones, the first and most direct is over-hunting, or killing animals faster than they can breed. This is chiefly how we have eliminated big animals, from mammoths 10,000 years ago to California grizzly bears this past century. And we are not yet finished. We no longer depend on such animals for meat, but we kill elephants for ivory and rhinos for their horns. At current rates of slaughter, not just elephants and rhinos but most other populations of large African and Southeast Asian mammals will be extinct (outside game parks and zoos) in a decade or two.

The second method of extermination is more indirect but no less effective: introducing species to parts of the world where they didn't previously exist. When such newcomers spread, they frequently kill off native species because the victims have no natural defenses. In the United States, for example, an introduced fungus has almost exterminated the American chestnut tree, just as on oceanic islands around the world, goats and rats have exterminated many native plants and birds. Although we might try to keep from introducing pests to new parts of the world, they will inevitably keep pace with human travel and commerce.

Meanwhile, new pests show up disguised as friends. In Africa's Lake Victoria a large fish called the Nile perch is now eating its way through the lake's hundreds of remarkable fish species. The Nile perch was intentionally introduced in a misguided effort to establish a new fishery. It will probably ring up the biggest number of extinctions caused by an introduced predator in modern times.

Destruction of habitat is the third path to extinction. Most species live in only one type of habitat: marsh wrens in marshes, pine warblers in pine forests. Many are even more particular, especially in the tropics. Centinela Ridge is an isolated habitat because it just reaches the clouds; before it was cleared, it was a unique "cloud forest" separated by valleys from similar habitats. When we cut such forests, we eliminate the local species almost as certainly as by shooting each individual. When all the forest on Cebu Island in the Philippines was logged, nine of the ten bird species unique to Cebu became extinct, and that last one may not survive.

The worst habitat destruction is still to come. We are just starting in earnest to destroy tropical rain forests. These forests cover only 6 percent of Earth's surface but harbor at least half of its species. Brazil's Atlantic forest and Malaysia's lowland forest are nearly gone, and most forests in Borneo and the Philippines will be logged within the next two decades. By the middle of the next century the only large tracts of tropical rain forest likely to be standing intact will be in parts of Zaire and the Amazon Basin.

Finally, our fourth method of extermination is by means of an inadvertent domino effect. Every species depends on many others, and often in such complex ways that it's impossible to foresee where any one extinction may ultimately lead. For example, when the Panama Canal created Gatun Lake in 1914 and turned Barro Colorado into an island, no one anticipated that the disappearance of jaguars and other big predators on that island would lead to the local extinction of little antbirds. But it did, because the big predators used to eat medium-size predators like peccaries, monkeys, and coatimundis. When the big predators disappeared, there was a population explosion of the medium-size predators, which proceeded to eat up the antbirds and their eggs.

A realistic projection for the future must take all these effects into account, as well as the knowledge that published lists of extinct and endangered species are gross underestimates. It is likely that more than half of all existing species will be extinct or endangered by the middle of the next century. If the estimate of 30 million for the world's total species is correct, then species are now becoming extinct at a rate of 150,000 per year, or 17 per hour.

Of course, there are people who dismiss the significance of these extinctions. So what if a few million beetle species disappear, they ask. We care about our children, not about bugs.

The answer is simply that, like all species, we depend on others for our existence. We need them to produce the oxygen we breathe, absorb the carbon dioxide we exhale, decompose our sewage, provide our food, and maintain the fertility of our soil.

Then couldn't we just preserve those species we need and let others become extinct? Of course not, because the species we need also depend on other species. The ecological chain of dominoes is much too complex for us to have figured out which dominoes we can dispense with. For instance, if you were the president of a timber company trying to figure out which species you could afford to let become extinct, you would have to answer these questions: Which ten tree species produce most of the world's paper pulp? For each of those ten tree species, which are the ten bird species that eat most of its insect pests, the ten insect species that pollinate most of its flowers, and the ten animal species that spread most of its seeds? Which other species do these birds, insects, and animals depend on?

Even without knowing the answers, you might be willing to take a chance. If you were trying to evaluate a project that would bring in millions of dollars but might exterminate a few obscure species, it would certainly be tempting to run the risk. But consider the following analogy. Suppose someone offers you a million bucks in return for the privilege of cutting out two ounces [60 g] of your valuable flesh. You might figure that two ounces [60 g] is less than one thousandth of your body weight, so you'll still have plenty left. That's fine if the two ounces [60 g] come from your spare body fat and if they'll be removed by a skilled surgeon. But what if the deal requires you to let anyone hack two ounces [60 g] from any conveniently accessible part of your body, the way much of the tropics are now being razed?

Am I saying, then, that our future is hopeless? Not at all. We are the ones who are creating the problem, so it's completely in our power to solve it. There are many realistic ways we can avoid extinctions, such as by preserving natural habitats and limiting human population growth. But we will have to do more than we are doing now.

If, on the other hand, we continue behaving as we have in the past, the devastation will also continue. The only uncertainty is whether we will halt the juggernaut or whether it will halt us.

Activities

1. With a partner, identify four methods of species extermination described in the essay. For each method, identify up to five species that are now extinct.

2. Select two sentences from the essay that you think contain important facts or ideas. Write a short explanation of the reasons why you find them important.

3. Since this is quite a long essay, reading might be facilitated by subdividing it into sections with their own headings. With a partner, decide how many sections there should be to the essay, where each one should begin and end, and what headings the subsections should have.

4. Write a journal entry explaining why you would or would not favour the extinction of the peskiest insect you know.

5. With a partner, research a plant or animal species that has become extinct. In your report, describe the habitat and interesting characteristics of the species. Evaluate the benefit or loss to the world of that species. Report your findings to the class.

6. In a journal entry,
   a) write about a natural resource in your community that has been lost to development and explain why you feel it should have been preserved

   OR

   b) describe some natural resource in your community that you hope will never be lost.

7. As a class, brainstorm situations in which the well-being of humans and the well-being of nature seem to be in conflict. Individually, research one of these situations and write a report outlining the nature of the conflict. Offer your opinion about which side's interest should take precedence.

8. In a group of three, brainstorm the names of plants or animals in the world that you think are endangered. Select one of these and make a poster that will raise the interest and concern of your fellow students in the problem. Information and sample posters are available from World Wildlife Fund (Canada) or Wildlife Preservation Trust Canada.

Controversy Corner

Battle Over Earth's Lesser Creatures

Miro Cernetig

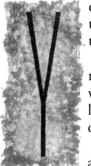

eehaw! It is rodeo season in the Canadian West, time again for cowboys in dusty denim to prove their mastery over the Earth's lesser creatures.

Like the bullfights of Spain, it is a pageantry rich in machismo; an arena in which young men with silvery, over-sized belt buckles can breathe life into a bit of the past that might otherwise only be found in dime-store Westerns.

Nowhere is this bucolic spectacle as grand as at the Calgary Stampede, the world's largest rodeo, unabashedly billed as the "Greatest Outdoor Show on Earth." For 10 days every summer, the grandstand rumbles as thousands of fans yip and holler at cowboys far below bucking and riding for a share of glory and a purse worth more than $500,000.

But like the bullfight, the rodeo is not without controversy. Sometimes, as Ernest Hemingway wrote of the bullring, there is a death in the afternoon.

"It's brute against brute," says Jake Yaskiw, one of six special constables who inspect some of the province's hundreds of rodeos for the Alberta Society for the Prevention of Cruelty to Animals. "Only, here, everything is stacked in favor of the cowboy.

"Sometimes animals will break their necks, or get a leg caught in the stall and snap it in half. They squeal. They make their painful noises. Sometimes you see the bones sticking out of the flesh."

This is a world still dominated by the Old Testament view that humans must conquer the wilderness and its beasts. That edict helped fuel the settlement of the North American West and still attracts young and old to the arduous life of the rodeo circuit.

On a typical day at the Calgary Stampede, cowboy heroes ride bucking horses and fearsome one-tonne Brahma bulls (with their horns blunted); they saddle wild horses, wrestle steers to the ground and then limp around slapping dust out of their faded Levis.

But modern values are encroaching on the rodeo. Today, old-time cowpokes say, people seem more worried about a cow crossing the great divide (as they call death) than a cowboy.

The SPCA and most humane societies in Canada and the United States are opposed to rodeos, which they believe cause animals stress and pain as well as mortal injuries.

"It's really quite barbaric," says Joy Ripley, president of the Alberta chapter of the SPCA. "There are really no events at the rodeo where animals don't get killed. As far as I'm concerned one dead animal is one too many."

And that is why Mr. Yaskiw, a Manitoba farmboy and former RCMP constable, is at the Stampede, watching the cowboys and the animals from behind his aviator sunglasses.

Although he is a soft-spoken, easy-going sort who gave up the RCMP for the SPCA because he thought the animals would appreciate the help more, his badge does not make him a popular figure at the rodeo. One cowboy brushed by him, warning bluntly that he'd better keep his distance or he, not the animals, would be put down.

But Mr. Yaskiw soldiers on, scribbling in his notebook whenever he sees an animal in distress. Even at the Calgary Stampede, widely considered one of the best run and safest rodeos in Canada, this does not take long. In fact, says Mr. Yaskiw, you generally only have to watch the wild horse race to understand how brutal rodeos can be.

In this event, 16 horses unaccustomed to saddles or humans are released into the corral where 16 three-man teams are waiting with the aim of saddling and riding them. In theory, this is accomplished by having one man from each team put his fingers up the horse's nostrils and bite its ear. Thus compromised, each horse is supposed to refrain from bucking or kicking, enabling the rest of the trio to place the saddle without being discombobulated.

But recently, a wild stallion was so frightened by the surroundings it bucked in the chute, hammering its head and legs against the steel as it tried desperately to escape. When released, it panicked, running blindly into another horse that pummelled it with its hooves.

At the end, it was led away, bleeding profusely from the tops of its eyes, while Mr. Yaskiw shook his head.

"Who do you feel sorry for?" he asked, pointing at one limping cowboy. "Him or the horse?"

Such events are lost to the majority of the more than 300,000 people who will have filed in to see the rodeo events and chuck-wagon contests by the time the Stampede finishes. By yesterday morning [July 13, 1990], three of the 2,000 animals involved had been killed.

"The public doesn't see the killing. They don't use guns in the arena to put them down," explained Mr. Yaskiw. "The animal ambulance takes them backstage and they are killed by lethal injection."

The SPCA, which can only investigate a few of the rodeos throughout the province, fears many more deaths take place at smaller rodeos.

Although statistics are hard to come by, the SPCA has one it says shows what the animals are up against. In three years of attending chuckwagon races, involving covered wagons and teams of horses and often likened to Roman chariot racing, SPCA officers reported 24 major accidents in 58 races, forcing nine animals to be destroyed.

"What," asks Ms. Ripley, "has that got to do with good herdsmanship or life on the ranch?"

Questions from an outsider about the treatment of animals are generally not welcomed by the cowboys (and cowgirls.) Most will look at you with suspicion. Some will tell you if a horse bucks in a chute and hurts itself, it is the horse's fault.

"You can't blame the man for what an animal does," says Vicki Adams, who rides a trick horse called Little Indian at the Stampede. "Nobody takes care of our animals better than we do. When they ran free on the open range, they didn't live long. They were prey to predators and disease."

Behind the scenes, where tired cowboys grab cans of Budweiser from a large ice-filled cooler, there is a muted bitterness over the attention focused on the animals by groups such as the SPCA. What, many wonder, about the cowboy?

The rodeo is continuously moving to improve its image. Occasionally, riders are fined or suspended for mistreatment of animals and a veterinarian is always on hand at the Stampede, though not at most rodeos.

Activities

1. With a partner, discuss your responses to the following questions:
   - What is the topic of the essay?
   - What is the author's attitude toward the topic?
   - What is the author's conclusion?

2. With a partner, think of three ways in which animals are used for entertainment that upset animal rights activists. Report these uses to the class indicating whether you agree or disagree with the activists and why.

3. Write a journal entry on one of the following:
   - a pet you have now or once had and what it means or meant to you
   - why you do or do not consider yourself an animal lover
   - why you would or would not ride in the Calgary Stampede if you had the opportunity

4. Arrange for a representative from the local humane society to visit your class. Have the person discuss with you the most common problems that occur regarding the treatment of animals in your community.

5. In your school or local library, research an article that focusses on animal rights. Write a brief synopsis of the article. At the end of the report, give your opinion on the issue presented in the article.

Where the Wild Things Are

Cathy Spencer

ings beating against the sky, a V-shaped flock of snow geese migrates southward. We humans, tethered to the earth, marvel at their airborne symmetry. These birds chart their course unerringly—relying on the sun and stars as guideposts, navigating thousands of miles from summer breeding grounds to winter habitats. Do the birds travel as one only by chance? Or is their journey evidence of evolution's hand?

Birds flock, fish school, wildebeests live in herds. Elephants, African and otherwise, congregate, welcoming a stray back to the fold with a community dance. Even the lone bald eagle will allow the company of others under certain conditions. These social patterns are part of a grand design: Species that stay together do so to ensure their survival—to guarantee the continuation of the gene pool. Many creatures, great and small, reproduce more successfully and are better protected when they live in groups. While some birds flock during migration, other aviators gather at specific sites solely to feed. Along the Pacific coasts of Canada and Alaska, for instance, large numbers of bald eagles assemble where salmon die after spawning. Because little competition for the food supply exists, the eagles put up with one another. Once sated, the birds embark on their singular peregrinations.

Certain breeds seem almost to enjoy a sense of community: Penguins travel together in flocks, tobogganing on their bellies across the ice as they migrate, making for a spectacular winter carnival. Especially gregarious, they perform elaborate vocalizations while convening on the frigid shores of Antarctica—in rookeries of up to 1 million. Their shore leave, however, occurs on the rarest of occasions (when they breed and molt, though not necessarily in that order).

The lesser flamingo (yes, there are greater flamingos, too) clusters nearly all the time. Thousands of couples prepare to mate simultaneously; this ensures rapid and synchronized egg laying. Though exhibitionists, preening and courting each other in public, they do appear to be monogamous.

Even the lowly marine iguanas, which sun themselves in groups, can be social when it's to their advantage: Courtship consists of the male bobbing his head and reaching for the female's neck. The rest is (natural) history. The giant tortoise's sexual contact is limited: It's possible for a female to mate only once and, because she stores the male's sperm in her body, then lay eggs for several years. (The mating, extremely rigorous, is also mighty unpleasant: Males bite, inflicting serious wounds on their beloveds, which attempt to flee.) They will take to the water together, though not for any specific purpose.

In the kingdom of animals sometimes a brood consists of blood relatives; other times the collection is as random as a group of moviegoers. A strange circle of aunts, uncles, mothers, and fathers surround African lion cubs. A group of sisters and a group of brothers from completely different genetic lines form a pride of lions. The reproductive cycles of all the females become synchronized within the pride; they go into heat and give birth at generally the same time. Females nurse both their own and their sisters' offspring. Because the females mate with several males, it's impossible to determine a cub's real father. As a result, each male treats every cub as if it were his own.

The gray wolf resides in a more traditional family unit. The parents—the alpha, or dominant, male and female—represent the only wolves in the pack that reproduce. Offspring of the alpha pair make up the rest of the family—as many as ten animals. Other wolf relatives, like maiden aunts, sometimes latch on to the pack and help with nurturing and hunting chores, creating an extended family. A single pair of wolves would have great difficulty feeding the young, thus jeopardizing the future of their gene pool. A family of wolves, however, works as a team and can thus down larger animals, usually moose or deer, substantial enough to meet the nutritional needs of the entire clan. (Young ones eat first; older siblings and adults follow.)

The survival of the African elephant (the shape of its ear imitates the shape of the land it hails from) depends less on the availability of food than on the vulnerable nature of a small group of animals living closely together. Traditionally, elephants collect in families made up of a mother, her daughters, their young, and sometimes a grandmother. Most of these females stay in the same herd for life—life being as long as 60 or 70 years. When males reach maturity at 14 to 16 years, however, the females drive them away in an effort to protect the rest of the group. Males then begin a life of solitary wandering, interrupted only by brief (though close) encounters with female elephants.

Within the hierarchy of the elephant family, a single female, usually the oldest animal, assumes the role of leader. She best understands the idiosyncrasies of the range—where it will provide food and where the terrain is unforgiving—and the herd depends on her knowledge for survival. The rest of the animals spend their time caring for one another and teaching the young.

Because of constant contact among animals, the elephants develop close social ties. Consequently, the sudden death of an individual disrupts the entire herd. With their agile trunks, the elephants will go over the body of the deceased, as if to determine the cause of death. When elephants are allowed to die naturally, the herd will sometimes hold a funeral, blanketing the body with mud and leaves, branches, and earth.

In parts of Africa where poaching is rampant, the family units have fallen apart and large herds of as many as 500 animals have formed. In the past, these large numbers offered a defense against predators. Unfortunately, this ancient instinct does not protect the elephants from rifles.

More than just elephants have been faced with slaughter; the killing of seal pups has enraged people the world over. Their vulnerability is brought home by the term *weaners*, meaning, of course, that they've only recently been separated from their mothers.

Zebras, too, were once hunted for their skins; these benign creatures, when left alone, will graze peacefully with other species, collecting at watering holes in herds as large as 10,000 during the rainy season. Within the herds, there are cliques of sorts: stallions that cavort together; families that nurture their own young, encouraging the newborns to keep pace with the adults at speeds up to 40 miles [64 km] per hour.

Strong bonds are forged among a gaggle of Canadian snow geese, whose homing instincts lead them over the same migratory path from generation to generation. For the females in particular, biology and destiny are linked; they prefer to return to their birthplace when breeding. On migratory trips, they draw together, but when summer arrives they prefer to wander in pairs.

Why do creatures living below the surface of rivers, lakes, and oceans gather together? That is, why do fish school?

Not all fish school. Some species live in kelp beds, hide in the sand, or live on coral reefs. Schooling best suits fish living in the open, where they are vulnerable to predators. A school is meant to befuddle intruders; when finding a lone fish, predators know exactly what to attack. But when confronted with a whole mass of fish, acting as a superorganism, the attacker becomes confused.

Schooling also works to communicate the presence of food and encourages fish to eat. Food appears sporadically and must be eaten before it floats or swims away.

To make sure they get their fill, still other water dwellers will run for their supper. The Sally Lightfoot crab, also a clusterer, will skip across short stretches of water (hence the name) en route to a seaweed dinner; disturb it and the crustacean squirts water at the interloper.

The habits of many of these beings are not so different from our own. Like elephants, we form family bonds and grieve for lost members. Like lions and seals, we nurture our young.

Should, in some fantasy world, these creatures have the chance to observe us, to chart our daily and nightly activities, they'd see us feeding in groups, commuting en masse, and in small towns at dusk, they would watch our offspring skipping lightly toward dinner. As Earth Day [April 22] approaches, it's fitting to pause and ponder the significance of each living thing. Somehow its survival is bound up with our own. And evident or not, a contribution to the world as a whole is made, by these and its millions of other inhabitants.

Activities

1. In a journal entry, explain which one of the examples presented in this essay seem most similar to human behaviour.

2. Write out the thesis of this essay in a sentence that begins "In this essay the author is trying to prove that..." In your own words, explain whether the essay effectively proves this thesis.

3. With a partner, identify three places in the essay where the author gives evidence that she has researched her topic.

4. In your journal, describe an activity that you prefer to do with several other people rather than alone. Comment on whether you think animals such as the ones described in this article enjoy doing things in groups for the same reasons.

5. With a partner, research an animal that interests you. Prepare a report for the class on any aspect(s) of the animal's behaviour that, in your opinion, offers humans a lesson about life.

6. Reread the last paragraph of the essay. As an animal writing material for an "animal encyclopedia," prepare entries about two strange or interesting types of behaviour observed in the human species. At the end of the entries, where the name of the author would ordinarily appear, identify the animal that did the observing and wrote the article.

7. With a partner, examine a children's book about animals. Prepare a report to a parent explaining whether you think the book would appeal to children and whether it would help children to understand and respect animals.

Point/Counterpoint

Do We Need to Use Animals in Research?

(Pro) Jane McCabe
(Con) Roger Caras

Pro

 see the debate about using animals in medical research in stark terms. If you had to choose between saving a very cute dog or my equally cute, blond, brown-eyed daughter, whose life would you choose? It's not a difficult choice, is it? My daughter has cystic fibrosis. Her only hope for a normal life is that researchers, some of them using animals, will find a cure. Don't misunderstand. It's not that I don't love animals, it's just that I love Claire more.

Nine years ago I had no idea that I would be joining the fraternity of those who have a vital interest in seeing that medical research continues. I was a very pregnant woman in labor; with my husband beside me I gave birth to a 7-pound, 1-ounce [3200-g] daughter. It all seemed so easy. But for the next four months she could not gain weight. She was a textbook case of failure to thrive. Finally a hospital test of the salt content in her sweat led to the diagnosis of cystic fibrosis.

The doctor gave us a little reason for hope. "Your daughter will not have a long life, but for most of the time, it will be a good life. Her life expectancy is about 13 years, though it could be longer or shorter. As research continues, we're keeping them alive longer."

"As research continues." It's not a lot to rely on but what's our alternative? We haven't waited passively. We learned how to take care of our little girl; her medical problems affect her digestion and lungs. We protected her from colds, learned about supplemental vitamins and antibiotics. We moved to California where the winters aren't so harsh and the cold and flu season isn't so severe. Our new doctor told us that the children at his center were surviving, on the average, to age 21. So far, our daughter is doing well. She is a fast runner and plays a mean first base. She loves her friends and is, in general, a happy little girl. All things considered, I feel very lucky.

How has research using animals helped those with CF? Three times a day my daughter uses enzymes from the pancreas of pigs to digest her food. She takes antibiotics tested on rats before they are tried on humans. As an adult, she will probably develop diabetes and need insulin—a drug developed by research on dogs and rabbits. If she ever needs a heart-lung transplant, one might be possible because of the cows that surgeons practiced on. There is no animal model to help CF research, but once the CF gene is located, new gene-splicing techniques may create a family of mice afflicted with the disease. Researchers would first learn to cure the mice with drugs, then cautiously try with humans.

There are only about 10,000 people with CF in the United States. But the number of people dependent on research is much larger. Walk with me through Children's Hospital at Stanford University: here are the youngsters fighting cancer, rare genetic illnesses, immunological diseases. Amid their laughter and desperate attempts to retain a semblance of childhood, there is suffering.

I think the motivation of animal-rights activists is to cut down on the suffering in this world, but I have yet to hear them acknowledge that people—young and old—suffer, too. Why is a laboratory rat's fate more poignant than that of an incurably ill child?

There are advocates for animals who only seek to cut down on "unnecessary research." They don't specify how to decide what is unnecessary, but they do create an atmosphere in which doing medical research is seen as distasteful work. I think that's wrong. Researchers should be thanked, not hassled.

Every time I see a bumper sticker that says "Lab animals never have a nice day," a fantasy plays in my brain. I get out of my car, tap on the driver's window and ask to talk. In my fantasy, the other driver gets out, we find a coffee shop and I show her photos of my kids. I ask her if she has ever visited Children's Hospital. I am so eloquent that her eyes fill with tears and she promises to think of the children who are wasting away as she considers the whole complicated issue of suffering.

I have other fantasies, too, that a cure is found for what ails my daughter, that she marries and gives us some grandchildren, and does great work in her chosen profession, which at this moment appears to be cartooning or computer programming. We can still hope—as long as the research continues.

Con

 believe that animals have rights which, although different from our own, are just as inalienable. I believe animals have the right not to have pain, fear or physical deprivation inflicted upon them by us. Even if they are on the way to the slaughterhouse, animals have the right to food and water and shelter if it is needed. They have the right not to be brutalized in any way as food resources, for entertainment or any other purpose.

Since animals must be classified as property if we are to have the power of life and death over them (and we must, even over our pets), there is a vast philosophical/legal rift to be negotiated. No other property has rights, yet animals must. It is going to take some fine legal minds to work out the details so that we can get across that gulch.

One of the most difficult problems is our unrelenting use of animals in biomedical research. Until recently the arguments between biomedical researchers and the humane movement centered on the conditions under which laboratory animals are maintained. Lately, in keeping with our "age of activism," it has become a raging name-calling contest over whether one species, ours, has the right to use other species to solve our own health problems. If tens of millions of people elect to smoke and expose themselves to the risks of cancer and heart disease, do we have the right to subject animals that would never smoke to those same cancers and heart diseases?

A great many researchers I have met would love to have alternatives. They are against vivisection in spirit but believe that today's research protocols require—and grant money goes to—research involving animals. Often they are right. What's more, the use of animals in research is not limited to the good of humans. Vaccines used on animals were developed using animals. Animal-rights advocates who decry using animals for research on human diseases have not made it clear what models should have been used for canine distemper, parvovirus or feline leukemia.

Animal-rights activists say that far too little effort has gone into seeking substitute methods such as cell culture and computer modeling. They are right. Finding a substitute for animals in research has only recently become an imperative in the scientific community. And that change has coincided with a change in the techniques employed by the militant animal-rights movement. When leaflets and picket signs were replaced by high raiders and bombers, science sat up and paid attention. Personally, I decry terrorism as the solution to any problem.

Many laboratories provide too little in the way of creature comforts (no pun intended) for laboratory animals. That has to change and in many places it is. Jane Goodall has fought to upgrade the psychological environment provided for chimpanzees. For an animal as bright as a chimp (its genetic package varies from our own by no more than 1 percent, most researchers agree), boredom and lack of social interaction is nothing less than cruelty according to Goodall.

Much of the research done on chimps involves their immune systems, current work on AIDS being an obvious example. Since scientists know that stress alters any animal's power to respond to invading organisms, why do they stress chimps by confining them in isolation when the research protocol doesn't demand it?

What has happened is analogous to current geopolitical problems. Everybody is so angry at everybody else nobody is really listening. The animal-rights groups are at odds with each other. That could be because they are all looking for the same membership dollars, the same bequests. Then, of course, there are the antivivisectionists vs. the provivisectionists. They are so busy shrieking at each other no one can be heard.

One day animals will not be used in the laboratory. How soon that day comes depends on how soon people stop screaming and make the search for alternatives a major research imperative. As long as conferences on the subject sound like feeding time at the monkey house, monkeys along with millions of other animals are going to stay right where they are now—in the laboratory.

Activities

1. In a journal entry, explain which of the two essays you most agree with and why. Refer to arguments presented in the essay that influenced your choice.

2. Debate the following: Be it resolved that using animals in research for the purpose of improving the quality of human life is acceptable.

3. In a group of three, locate a copy of the Canadian Charter of Rights. Using it as a model, draw up a Charter of Rights for Animals. Share it with other groups.

4. With a partner, list the topic sentence for each paragraph in the essay by Roger Caras. Discuss whether you think the list is a clear outline of the essay. Make changes to the sentences if you feel they could be improved. Compare your list and ideas with other partnerships.

A Touch of Humour

Boutique Gives Dogs a Chance to Dress Up Like Their Owners

iffany models a shimmering golden-white gown as she poses for the photographer. Her misty brown eyes reflect a sequinned veil which falls from a majestic crown perched atop her curly head.

Tiffany, who is clearly enjoying herself, is a dog.

"Tiffany loves to dress up," said her owner, Mavis Dustow. "Like most toy poodles, she loves attention."

Nearby, two other poodles dressed in deep blue and purple Klondike costumes are barking loudly, eager to catch the photographer's eye.

"The others get so jealous when they're not the centre of attention," Dustow said.

Dustow and her husband, Harvey, operate Sivam Poodle Boutique, which features an extensive selection of originally designed outfits for poodles and other dogs. Wedding outfits like those worn by Prince Charles and Diana, Ultrasuede winter coats lined with imitation mink, jogging pyjamas and various ethnic costumes are among the selection. The average price for an outfit is about $30. Costumes for large dogs cost about $85.

The three-year-old boutique was originally a grooming service for dogs. But the Dustows decided to include clothing after requests from customers.

Poodles have long been part of Dustow's life. She has groomed dogs for 20 years and has entered about 70 poodles in championship competitions.

The shop features a few outfits imported from Texas, but most are made by an Edmonton dressmaker. "We did start with designer outfits from the United States, but we found out that the clothing we could make ourselves is much superior."

There are also goods such as perfumed-scented shampoos, colognes and brushes.

"Almost anything you want for a dog can be made to order," Dustow said.

The strangest order came last summer from a client who wanted four dresses for her poodles who were going to be part of a bridal party. Dustow said she was initially puzzled by the request but when she saw the wedding pictures "it looked quite nice."

Dustow doesn't think dressing up poodles is ridiculous, although she's had to face some criticism from people who believe a dog's place is in the backyard.

"I think most people enjoy their pets just as much as they do their children," she said. "I'm a firm believer that God put these beautiful little creatures on earth for us to enjoy, not to be put outside."

And, "at least they can't talk back."

Activities

1. After rereading the last line of the essay, select one of the poodles described in the article and write its response to the clothes it wears.

2. In a journal entry, write your opinion about dressing pets in outfits such as the ones described in this article.

3. Design a product for a pet and present it to the class in the form of a television or radio commercial.

4. Visit a pet shop or pet care centre in your community to observe the variety of items for sale. Report about some of the items you found most unusual to your classmates.

5. With a partner, find an article in a magazine, a newspaper, or the vertical files on the therapeutic value of pets. A data base might be of assistance. Report the contents of the article to your class. As a class, brainstorm a list of the positive effects of pets in the lives of their owners.

End of Unit Activities

1. Write a report about the animal you would most like to study if you were to become a zoologist. Learn the name given to the study of that animal. Make a summary of your report and share it with classmates.

2. With a partner, research the cost and care involved in owning and caring for two different animals. Prepare a booklet about the care of these creatures to include in your class library.

3. With a partner, research a plant or animal that has been "improved" by scientific methods. In a report to the class on your findings, offer your evaluation of this scientific activity. You might check a data base such as the CBCA (Canadian Business and Current Affairs) under *bio-technology* and *genetic engineering* to locate information.

4. Watch an episode of a nature show on television. Prepare an oral report to the class about one or two interesting facts on the creatures highlighted.

5. Prepare a book for a preschooler that both describes an animal and encourages the child to develop a sense of respect for this form of life.

6. Stage a debate on one of the following resolutions. Research may be necessary.
   - Be it resolved that humans are necessarily in conflict with the rest of nature.
   - Be it resolved that animals should not be killed to provide food and clothing for humans.
   - Be it resolved that humans should not interfere with the process of natural selection.

7. Write an essay on one of the following topics. Research may be necessary.
   - the importance of respect for all forms of life
   - the role of animals in research and development of new products and medicines for human use
   - the difference between animal instinct and human intelligence and why they are sometimes confused

The Green Planet

It has always seemed to me to be simplicity itself to raise money for things which are of doubtful help to our planet. Most conservation organizations run around after funds like a starving dog after a bone, and their laudable object is to try to save something from the debris of the world. But should you want money to buy a nuclear bomb or two, the funds are miraculously forthcoming.

GERALD DURRELL,
ANIMAL STORY WRITER

The beauty of the trees,
the softness of the air,
the fragrance of the grass
speaks to me.
. . . .
And my heart soars.

CHIEF DAN GEORGE,
ACTOR

For the first time in the history of the world, every human being is now subjected to contact with dangerous chemicals from the moment of conception until death.

RACHEL CARSON,
ECOLOGICAL ACTIVIST

Pollution control, like charity, must begin at home.

MARGARET ATWOOD,
WRITER

The Last Wilderness: Images of the Canadian Wild

David Suzuki

 ur species' evolutionary ancestors descended from the trees perhaps twenty million years ago. Our bipedal forebears moved onto the great plains of Africa, where for millions of years they shared their living space with countless other animals and plants on whom they depended not only for survival but also for companionship. We are linked to all other organisms through the long sweep of evolutionary history embedded in our DNA. I believe there is as well a genetic record of our companionship with them and thus the human need for wilderness is real, profound and biological.

Homo sapiens' key survival trait has been our remarkable ability to adapt to novel environments through the flexibility and inventiveness of our brain. Ever since the agricultural revolution some ten millennia ago, there has been a growing concentration of people in permanent settlements and a subsequent reshaping of the world around us. Now most Canadians, indeed most of the entire industrialized world, live in urban settings or in rural areas that are highly groomed and shaped according to human specifications.

Today most of us experience wilderness in parks—highly managed areas complete with electrical outlets, cut wood, garbage bins and, in heavily used areas, even shower and laundry facilities. Modern campers share the experience with others and can seldom escape the blare of a portable radio or the honk of a car's horn. Wilderness, as it was experienced by all human beings for ninety-nine percent of our species' existence, is an increasingly rare and precious experience.

Canadians possess a disproportionate share of remaining places on the planet that are untouched by humans. Europe has long been transformed by deforestation and agriculture. Already most of the old-growth forests in the eastern half of Canada have been logged, while the boreal forests of the prairie provinces appear headed for massive pulp mills. Like the Amazon rain forest, coastal Canadian rain forests are being cleared faster than they can be replaced. These magnificent ecosystems have the capacity to support three times the bio-density of the Amazon, and the great Sitka spruce, cedar and Douglas fir trees have been likened to the whales of the world's forests. These unique and irreplaceable watersheds appear ready to disappear within this generation. These forests are symptomatic of what is happening to wilderness throughout the world.

Around the planet, wilderness is being reduced to mere vestiges in parks and reserves. At current rates of destruction, only two large and two smaller untouched tracts of wilderness, all in Third World tropical countries, will remain by the end of the century. Disappearance of the forests is accompanied by extinction of the life forms that inhabit them. As tropical rain forests disappear at the horrifying rate of an acre [0.4 ha] a second, scientists like Harvard's E. O. Wilson estimate some 22,000 species of plants and animals also disappear annually. Each year, our world becomes a radically poorer place as species diversity becomes ever more restricted.

Most justifications for the preservation of biodiversity in wilderness areas are based on economic and utilitarian arguments. Thus, we have barely begun to tap the potential of plants and animals for their medicinal qualities. The best example is the periwinkle plant from Madagascar in which a potent anti-leukemia agent has been found. Most of human-kind lives on twenty domesticated species of plants of which three grasses—rice, corn and wheat—are the most important. Yet there are at least 50,000 species of plants known to be edible and many far superior nutritionally to the ones now in use. Many trees can be logged in a sustainable way if done selectively and carefully. Numerous nuts, fruits and fibres can be harvested indefinitely without destroying forests. As well,

there is potential in forests for sport and tourism. All of these arguments for the retention of forests are valid but remain founded on the human imperative to exploit a resource for our species' benefit. Even our concern about the impact of the destruction of tropical rain forests on weather, climate and global warming suggests hazards to humans as the main reason to stop the destruction.

But in the end, the profound reason for recognizing the value of wilderness is *spiritual*. We have become like a cancer within the body of the aggregate of life that some call Gaia. Human inventiveness, long the key to our survival, has been harnessed as science and technology, and now allows us to

extract resources far beyond their replaceability. And so we have temporarily escaped the constraints of a finite planet and believe the illusion that we lie outside of nature and have the knowledge to dominate and control it.

We are no longer *of* the earth but astride it. Driven by an economic imperative to grow and maximize profit, we no longer have a horizon that encompasses future generations. As industrialized *Homo sapiens*, we have lost our roots and sense of place—we have no home. Until we rediscover our kinship with the rest of life and come to revere and respect it, we will deny our biological need for nature and continue our destructive rampage.

Activities

1. Prepare a poster illustrating a diagram of this essay. Place the title of the essay in the centre and the topic sentences of the paragraphs spreading out from the centre.

2. In a group of three, discuss what David Suzuki means by the economic, utilitarian, and spiritual arguments for preserving wilderness areas. Decide which argument is the most convincing to you. Share the reasons for your choice with another group.

3. Identify the distinction David Suzuki draws between urban, rural, and wilderness areas. Write a description of the environment in which you feel most comfortable. In a second paragraph, explain how your choice affects your attitude about the preservation of wilderness areas in the country.

4. Locate a newspaper or magazine article that focusses on the issue of a vanishing wilderness. You could research material in library vertical files or a data base. Write a summary of the information in the article and be prepared to share it with the class.

5. Prepare a bulletin board display of problems and proposed solutions to the vanishing forest regions of Canada and other parts of the world.

The Earth Is One Big System

Geoffrey Cowley

t's sometimes said that modern scientists are learning so much about so little that they'll eventually know everything about nothing. James Lovelock is troubled by that trend, and doing what he can to counter it. Instead of seeking a safe niche in a scientific subspecialty, the maverick chemist-biologist-inventor has spent two decades working on an all-encompassing theory of evolution—one that will explain not only how the camel got its hump and the peacock its plume but how the Earth came by its unique climate, chemistry and atmosphere.

In a new book, *The Ages of Gaia: A Biography of Our Living Earth*, Lovelock advances a thrilling possibility. He argues that life has evolved not just by adapting to its surroundings, as Darwin had it, but by remaking them. The reason the Earth is so different from Mars or Venus, he says, is that living things have taken control of it, have in effect transformed an inert chemical ball into an immense self-sustaining organism. Lovelock calls the living planet Gaia, after the Greek Earth goddess. And he insists that scientists will never begin to understand her until they start thinking of ecology, geology and chemistry just as physicians think of breathing and digestion: as mechanisms for keeping a larger system alive.

At the heart of Gaian theory, which Lovelock has been advocating since the early 1970s, is the fact that the land, water and air have all been changed in specific, observable ways by the presence of life. There was, for instance, virtually no oxygen in the atmosphere until 2 billion years ago, when the ancestors of modern plants started using photosynthesis to harness the sun's energy. Because photosynthesis produces the gas as a by-product, the spread of green things eventually created an atmosphere in which countless other new species could evolve. If the overall oxygen concentration ever changed significantly, life as we know it would grind to a halt. Yet for hundreds of millions of years now the world's photosynthesizers have held the blend at an ideal 21 percent.

Climate, too, has been dramatically affected by life. Just last year Lovelock and his colleagues published new evidence that tiny marine organisms have a hand in regulating global temperatures. It seems that some species of plankton produce a chemical called dimethyl sulfide, or DMS, which accumulates in the oceans and then diffuses into the atmosphere. Once airborne, DMS oxidizes, leaving behind sulfate particles that serve as the "condensation nuclei" from which many of the world's clouds are formed. The amount of DMS produced by plankton may affect the temperature of the planet by controlling the density of its heat-reflecting cloud cover.

Few scientists dispute these connections. In fact most now accept that life affects everything from rainfall to the salinity of the oceans—and they applaud Lovelock's ground-breaking insights into the specific processes involved. What has always bothered them is his insistence that living organisms don't merely influence their environment but work together "to keep it comfortable" for themselves. How, critics ask, could the world's slime molds, plankton and polar bears even perceive their effect on the planet, let alone coordinate their activities on a global scale?

Lovelock allows that reasonable people could disagree on whether life's influence extends to total control. But he denies that global regulation would require anything as ludicrous as a conspiracy among slime molds. He has always claimed that a seemingly willful and intelligent global system could arise *automatically* from the mindless struggle for individual survival. And he has recently proved it, at least in theory, by simulating the process on a computer.

Ecologists often use computer models to study processes that would take lifetimes to observe in nature. They may, for instance, place a population of foxes and rabbits in an imaginary environment and, by running out series of equations, see how each species will fare over thousands of generations. Lovelock's model works on the same general principle. Using only numbers, he conjures up a planet called Daisyworld and seeds it with two types of daisies—light ones and dark ones. While the sun grows steadily stronger, they compete to survive and reproduce over several eons. As in a conventional model, the dark daisies, with their capacity to absorb heat, flourish when the sun is weak. The light ones, which tend to reflect heat, predominate as the sun grows more intense.

But in Daisyworld, that's not all there is to ecology. When the sun is weak, the dark daisies tend to raise the global thermostat, by trapping whatever heat is available. When the sun is strong, the spread of light ones has the opposite effect, because it creates a reflective shield. Together, the light and dark daisies perform an amazing feat. As the sun grows more intense, their planet doesn't grow hotter, as it would in a conventional model. It grows whiter and more reflective—and its temperature remains essentially flat. When the sun finally becomes too strong for even the white daisies, they disappear and the temperature goes wild. But as long as there are daisies on the planet they work mindlessly to create a daisy-friendly environment.

The Earth is of course infinitely more complicated. The fate of real daisies depends not just on temperature but on the quality of the air and soil, not to mention the presence of foxes, rabbits and tall trees. Yet unlike the old models of ecology, Daisyworld doesn't fall apart when such factors are taken into account. In Lovelock's model—as on Earth—the most varied ecosystems are the most robust. "You can throw in as many species as you like," he says, "and it becomes more stable."

The Gaia hypothesis, with or without computer models, has always appealed to environmentalists. Lovelock himself expresses grave concern over humankind's wanton disruption of natural processes, but he takes a long view of the likely consequences. Nothing we do is likely to kill the planet, he says; over the past few billion years, Gaia has survived volcanic eruptions and meteor impacts that would "make total nuclear war seem, by comparison, as trivial as a summer breeze." The danger is that we'll deal ourselves, and a lot of other species, out of the game.

Consider what we're doing to the climate, he says. Our sun, like Daisyworld's, has grown 25 percent stronger over the past 3 billion years. Luckily for us, the amount of heat-trapping carbon dioxide in the atmosphere has declined over the same period, preventing a corresponding shift in temperature. The problem is that humankind is now doing just about everything possible to *raise* the carbon dioxide concentration: burning the fossil fuels that produce the gas, while destroying much of the rich tropical vegetation that removes it from the air.

The result could be that the tropics consist mainly of baked-clay deserts within a few decades, and global temperatures rise by 3 to 9 degrees. To Gaia, that would be a minor perturbation —nothing compared with the fit of volcanic and meteoric activity that some scientists believe blackened the skies, lowered the temperature and extinguished the dinosaurs 66 million years ago. But for humankind and others, it could be an unprecedented disaster. Gaia is a dynamic system, not a static one. It may always regain its balance, but it has no attachment to particular life forms. Ninety-nine percent of them have gone extinct.

Lovelock is disappointed that so few scientists have joined his quest for a larger theory of life and the planet. Trying to understand nature from the narrow perspective of ecology or geology is as senseless as trying to discern the purpose of sweat from its chemistry, he says. Yet tribal and institutional pressures keep modern scientists from looking beyond their specialties. Lovelock himself gave up university life years ago to conduct his research independently, at his home in the English countryside. "As a university scientist," he notes, "I would have found it nearly impossible to do full-time research on the Earth as a living planet."

No question about that. Yet he is no longer quite the outcast he likes to think. The Gaia hypothesis is gradually winning respect: it gets cited in scientific journals these days, and it's becoming a hot topic at mainstream scientific gatherings. A hundred years from now, Lovelock's theory may be remembered as a romantic's dream. But as the celebrated physician and writer Lewis Thomas is fond of noting, it may yet go down as one of the fundamental turning points in human thought. Lovelock himself isn't holding his breath. "New ideas follow a predictable progression," he says. "First people say, 'It's absurd!' Then they say, 'Maybe.' And finally they say, 'We knew it along.'"

Activities

1. Look up Gaia in an encyclopedia of Greek mythology. Write a brief report on the relationship between the Greek myth of Gaia and James Lovelock's theory.

2. With a partner, explain in your own words how the two kinds of daisies in Daisyworld create an environment in which there will always be daisies. Explain how this simple model helps to explain Lovelock's view of the world. Be prepared to explain your ideas to other students.

3. Write a journal entry in which you indicate how the ideas in the essay make you feel about the world and its future.

4. With a partner, decide whether the ideas developed in this essay are primarily rational and scientific or imaginative and poetic. Select two or three passages that support your point of view and discuss your conclusions with another partnership.

5. Obtain a copy of a photograph of the Earth from a NASA spaceship that shows the planet afloat in space and write a poem about your home planet. Arrange the photograph and your poem artistically on a poster to display on the bulletin board.

Garbage Blues

Carrie Buchanan

he old school gymnasium in Bristol, Que., is packed. Two hundred people fill the chairs and line the walls, spilling out the door at the back. Television lights add a harsh glare to the scene. At the front of the room are two dozen people wearing matching white sweatshirts with large lettering across the backs: Don't dump on us in Bristol!

It is June 15, 1987, and the Bristol township council is meeting in special session. The six councillors sit at desks on a dais, looking uncomfortable under the unaccustomed TV lights and microphones. In the middle is Mayor Jack Graham, an insurance salesman and hackney pony breeder. Graham became part-time mayor two years earlier, never expecting the job to be so demanding. But that was before the multinational Lavalin Corporation proposed to use an abandoned mine pit as a landfill dump for garbage from Ottawa and Hull, 70 kilometres away.

Like an electric shock, the Lavalin proposal in late 1985 galvanized this quiet rural community. Never in Bristol's history has there been such attendance at council meetings, with 50, 100 or more of the 1,085 permanent residents often turning out, and the 567 cottagers adding their numbers in summer.

Lavalin has worked hard to sell its plan. A team of four young people (two of them locals) visited every house in Bristol township during the four months prior to the meeting. Their boss, Gordon McGuinty, gave weekly talks at the mine site, with a slide show highlighting the sophisticated technology that would remove methane gas and leachate (rain and meltwater that has percolated through the dump) and emphasizing the 92 jobs the project could create in the economically depressed area (565 applications have been received).

Nevertheless, Bristol's council has resolutely opposed the project, resisting a lucrative offer of monthly royalties from Lavalin and ignoring preliminary site approval from Quebec's Ministère de l'environnement. In a classic case of the mouse taking on the lion, this tiny township has used its local zoning power to hold the mighty Lavalin at bay.

The people of Bristol are afraid of ground-water pollution from chemicals leaching out of the landfill. Since many use well water, some of them dairy farmers who use hundreds of litres daily and are uneasy about the possible effect on their herds, this is no minor concern. The cottagers whose summer homes line the river bank don't like Lavalin's plan to pump treated leachate into the Ottawa River. Others worry about 40 trucks a day transporting the garbage to the site. And many say the dump will spoil the scenic beauty of Bristol.

Tonight's meeting is important. Lavalin has challenged the township's position, saying its door-to-door survey found many residents in favour of the landfill. The township has conducted its own poll, sending a questionnaire to all 1,130 landowners, cottagers included. The results are about to be announced.

When the mayor reads out the numbers, a loud cheer rises from the crowd. The results confirm what most people suspected: 83 percent oppose the landfill scheme; it's a clear victory. Only a few people—maybe two dozen—look dejected. Still, many non-land-owners who favour the dump did not come because the vote excluded them. Lavalin has 300 signed letters of support for the landfill, all from residents. And there are those 565 job applications.

Bristol was founded in 1846 by farmers settling on newly cleared land during the Ottawa River valley lumber boom. By the end of the century, thousands of hectares of virgin pine forest had been felled and floated down the Ottawa to lumber and paper mills in communities lining its banks. With the land clearance, the Ottawa Valley became—and continues to be—a thriving agricultural region.

Bristol was also a mining town. In 1870, magnetite, an iron ore, was discovered and a mine operated intermittently from 1872 to 1894. Later, in 1956, it reopened as the Hilton iron ore mine, which blasted and chipped away the granite quarry, creating a 300-metre-deep, cone-shaped pit and a mountain of aggregate rock tailings. Ten years ago the mine closed, and since then surface drainage has created a small lake in the pit, now stocked with trout. To make it suitable for a dump, Lavalin proposes to install a shaft from top to bottom to pump the water out. The pump would remove leachate while the dump is active, and for 20 years after it is closed. This leachate would be treated and then discharged into the Ottawa River.

Lavalin has called the mine "one of the best sites in North America" for a landfill. A hydrogeological study (of water flow patterns and the geology of the locale) in 1985 designated the pit an "impervious quarry", clearly an ideal site. But Lavalin and the current owner, Maurice Lamarche, who was a partner with Lavalin until 1989, spent $1.2 million on studies and proposals for this property, and achieved almost nothing.

Once Lavalin came into the picture, the landfill venture dominated many council meetings in Bristol township. It has divided the community and made enemies of lifelong friends. Sally Keindel, one of the small group promoting the landfill for its economic benefits, says vindictive neighbours have made life miserable for her since she started to speak in favour of the dump, even kicking her off the school hot dog committee.

The bitterness spread in 1991, when Lamarche convinced the neighboring municipality of Pontiac to annex the mine, which lies on its border. Suddenly, Pontiac's council meetings were filled with angry residents, and Bristol's mayor and council asked the province to intervene and declare the annexation illegal. Officials were still pondering their decision in late 1991.

At the same time, Lamarche and McGuinty teamed up for a new venture in Kirkland Lake, Ontario, where they purchased another abandoned mine and convinced Metro Toronto to ship its garbage there by train. However, the provincial government intervened and killed the deal, saying no Ontario municipality would be allowed to export its garbage.

Meanwhile, Lavalin experienced serious economic difficulties and backed off from its joint venture with Lamarche in Bristol. Lavalin officials said in 1991 that if Lamarche succeeded in getting a permit to operate, from Bristol or Pontiac, it would consider reviving the joint venture, though its economic woes might make that impossible. Residents say they will not relax their vigilance, and they will continue to attend council meetings.

Throughout North America, rural communities, like Bristol, are being asked to accept urban refuse as increasing public anxiety in cities and towns about environmental dangers makes it difficult to find new landfill sites. With many rural economies in a slump, some townships find it tempting to take trash for cash.

Wherever new landfill sites are proposed, worried citizens are poring over hydrogeological studies and learning about the hazards of leachate, which may carry dissolved toxic chemicals down to the water table. The spectre of New York State's Love Canal, where toxic chemical seepage forced residents to abandon their homes in 1978, makes it nearly impossible nowadays to get public approval to bury wastes in the ground.

In Bristol, as in other communities, engineers offer elaborate plans to collect the leachate before it sinks into the ground. They say if they find a site with the right type of soil—clay or granite being ideal because they are almost impermeable—they can run drainage pipes around the periphery of the dump, collect the leachate (which runs sideways when it can't penetrate the ground underneath), and treat it using a water purification system to remove toxic chemicals, which will be sent to a toxic waste disposal facility. Although leachate collection systems have been installed at many dumps in the past decade, it can take many years for the water to percolate through. So it is not yet proved that this technique can prevent ground-water pollution.

Biologist Theresa Anískowicz, a Bristol resident and opponent of the Lavalin landfill, says the leachate treatment system doesn't impress her. "They're planning to treat only the 13 chemicals listed by the Ministry of the Environment." She worries about the ones that haven't been identified. Engineer Bill Cornfield, consultant to Ottawa's waste management task force, concedes that in 20 years the systems now in use will be considered primitive.

The fact remains, however, every week a truck picks up people's garbage. What's to be done with it?

Canadians generate about half a tonne of household garbage per person per year. Of this, a third or more is paper, another third is organic waste (food and yard refuse). The final third is made up of glass, metal, plastic, textiles, wood and "other"— about five percent in each category.

Cornfield works for MacLaren Engineering, a consulting firm owned by Lavalin Corporation. Lavalin (with 6,000 employees in 50 countries) has several corporate divisions devoted to waste management, from toxic chemicals to municipal landfills. Business is booming for waste management engineers these days. Cornfield believes there is a lot more to come as industry develops all sorts of schemes to turn waste materials into usable products and as it realizes that disposal projects can also make money. Two Canadian businesses attest to that money-making potential: Tricil Ltd., which builds and runs incinerators, and handles toxic wastes; and Laidlaw Waste Systems Ltd., which collects garbage and originated a curbside recycling program now operating in several Ontario cities.

Of course, money is crucial. Landfilling has always been cheap. As it becomes more expensive and less accepted, municipal politicians are looking for new ways to get rid of garbage. Waste management has become a major environmental issue, and one in which the public is becoming very much involved. In Ontario, the Environmental Assessment Act requires municipalities to study garbage disposal and develop "waste management master plans", with hearings and briefs from interested citizens. In Alberta, environmental hearings are standard procedure when a new landfill site or incinerator is under consideration.

As people learn more about waste management, they are discovering there are two alternatives to landfill dump sites: incineration and recycling. The first is being promoted by engineers and government officials at all levels, but the public has recently been frightened by reports that incineration pollutes the air with poisonous hydrocarbons (dioxins and furans). The second, recycling, is universally favoured but has faced a multitude of problems in practice, including costs, market fluctuations and obsolete equipment.

Modern incinerators, like the one in Parkdale, P.E.I., are called energy-from-waste plants because they produce steam or electricity as a by-product of burning garbage. Incineration proponents point to the efficiency of reducing waste by using garbage as an energy source.

In the early 1970s, the first of these incinerators were built in a wave of energy-conservation idealism in Hamilton, Montreal and Quebec City. But in the past 10 years, we have discovered that burning garbage creates dioxins and furans, both of which are formed when organic materials combine with chlorine, a component of many substances, from table salt to plastics.

In Hamilton, where a solid waste reduction unit incinerator has been operating since 1972, some $12-million worth of new equipment had to be installed to reduce dioxin and furan emissions as well as the ash particles that spewed out into the surrounding community. Even now [March 1988] that unit cannot guarantee the same low level of emissions as the newer plants. In Montreal and Quebec City, pollution controls on incinerators have cost between $10 million and $20 million.

Older incinerators have fared worse. Many municipal ones have been closed for not meeting increasingly stringent emission standards. However, many are still used in old apartment buildings and hospitals, which do not have special pollution control equipment.

Nonetheless, there is good news these days for incineration. The latest pollution control devices—scrubbers and fabric filters—have proven highly effective in removing toxic substances (although they remain in the ash which is buried in ordinary landfill) and such acidic gases as sulphur dioxide and hydrogen chloride. As a result, a new round of incinerator construction appears to be starting, with Vancouver and London, Ont., leading the way. Ottawa and Metropolitan Toronto considered incinerators, too, but were told by the provincial government in 1991 that there would be no provincial subsidies for incineration, because they were thought to discourage recycling and reuse. And the costs for incineration plants—which must be solid enough to sustain very high temperatures as well as contain built-in pollution control devices—are high; Ottawa had estimated $60 million for its proposed unit.

But no matter how sophisticated the technology, the environmental group, Pollution Probe, views incineration as an extravagant waste of energy which also interferes with conservation measures like recycling.

Pollution Probe argues that burning garbage is an inefficient way of producing energy; a study of 46 German incinerators, for example, showed only 20 percent of the energy originally in the garbage was ever recovered. Even if incinerators become more efficient, they would still be destroying substances that can be recycled.

Moreover, according to Pollution Probe, incineration and recycling are not compatible. Wherever incinerators flourish, they require almost all the garbage generated—particularly paper products—to maintain steady combustion. In Germany, cities that recycle from 50 percent to 65 percent of their waste do not have an incinerator.

"Recycling is the first law of waste management," says Duncan Bury, Ottawa's waste management coordinator. "Everybody's in favour of it." And why not? It is not dangerous, does not pollute, and it conserves energy.

But the road to recycling, though paved with good intentions, has not been straight or smooth. Until recently, recycling programs in Canada failed everywhere because they could not support themselves financially. Fredericton's curbside collection of newspapers and bottles, the only municipal recycling program in the Maritimes, was discontinued last May for that reason.

Today a new breed of waste managers is convincing the skeptical that recycling is a legitimate waste disposal method, not something to be relegated to the Boy Scouts as a fund raiser. Indeed, the Alberta Environment Council suggests that tax subsidies applied to recycling could make it cheaper than landfilling, and a great deal cheaper than incineration.

"Recycling programs have been severely undercapitalized, using beat-up old second-hand trucks and minimum-wage labour," says Paul Taylor of Resource Integration Systems, a Toronto firm specializing in waste management. "That has changed in Ontario. Probably the first truly professional program was the one in Kitchener."

There, in 1981, the city's garbage contractor, Laidlaw, presented every home with a bright blue plastic box with the slogan

"We Recycle" stamped on the sides. Weekly collection of tin cans, glass jars and newspapers began, and the sight of hundreds of blue boxes inspired the reluctant, embarrassed the lazy, and made it easy and convenient to participate. Kitchener boasts a participation rate of 85 percent, a level unheard-of before the boxes appeared.

Now [March 1988] there are 20 such programs in Ontario, as well as pilot projects in Edmonton, Ancienne-Lorette (a suburb of Quebec City) and LaSalle (near Montreal). In fact, the idea is catching on in more and more Canadian communities, and several American cities, including Boston, have started the blue-box system as well. In Ontario and elsewhere, the new programs have received a boost from progressive provincial legislation and generous subsidies.

A major influence in this new recycling drive has been the soft drink industry. Some provinces (Alberta, Saskatchewan, Quebec and Prince Edward Island) have deposit legislation, which applies to all soft drink containers. These deposits have ensured a high rate of return of both refillable and non-refillable containers; most of the latter (metal and plastic) are then recycled. Prince Edward Island prohibits non-refillables entirely, saying the island cannot sustain a recycling program.

In Ontario, however, soft drink manufacturers, allied with grocers and can manufacturers, are determined to prevent deposit legislation. Under 1985 regulations, 40 percent of soft drink containers had to be refillable. The Ontario government agreed that if 50 percent of the remaining (non-refillable) cans and bottles were recycled by November 1, 1988, there would be no deposit law and the 40 percent refillable requirement would be dropped to 30 percent. (This 50 percent target was achieved.) With this incentive, Ontario Multi-Materials Recycling Inc. was formed and spent $20 million to help municipal recycling programs get started. Of course, the municipal programs recycle newspapers, food cans and glass jars as well.

Another Ontario advantage is its markets. A diverse industrial base provides recyclers with bottlers and steel mills to buy glass and cans. With five bottle manufacturers, for example, Ontario can recycle glass from most regions, whereas British

Columbia has only one plant—in the Okanagan Valley. "Ontario has a tremendous edge," says Taylor, who for six years headed the Ontario Recycling Council.

Industry has sometimes been innovative about recycling its own wastes. The Canadian Waste Materials Exchange, started by Environment Canada and now operating nationally (it also has special branches in Ontario, Manitoba and Alberta), publishes a list of thousands of waste products generated by companies, which others might be able to use. It has led to hundreds of swaps, such as waste popcorn going to a pig farmer, and phenol, an unwanted by-product of oil refining, being bought by a plastics manufacturer. Not only do the owners of the waste product thus avoid having to pay to have the stuff carted away, they turn an unexpected dollar. It is estimated an exchange of 200,000 tonnes a year runs up about $6 million in sales.

Saving money, conserving energy and preserving the environment are powerful incentives for recycling. Self-interest is another important motivation. People who discover there might be a landfill or incinerator site near their homes become instant recycling advocates!

The days of vanishing garbage, when the trucks picked it up and it magically disappeared, are gone. Increasingly, cities are faced with toxic chemicals leaching from former city dumps and air pollution emanating from old incinerators. We are being forced to confront our garbage.

How we deal with it, now and in the future, says and will say a great deal about us. "By their garbage shall ye know them," says Christie Logan, town scavenger in Margaret Laurence's novel, *The Diviners*. "The Nuisance Grounds" is Christie's name for the town dump. It could be the name for Bristol's mine pit, or any other landfill site. It's a nuisance that will not go away.

Activities

1. With a partner, list information you learned from this essay and other knowledge you may have about the following topics:
   - garbage incineration
   - landfill sites
   - recycling programs

   Write your thoughts about an action you might take to help resolve one of the problems on your list.

2. Research information on the processing of garbage in your community. Find out how much garbage is produced, how and where it is disposed of, and what plans exist for controlling the production of garbage today and for disposing of it in the future.

3. Role play the Bristol township council meeting with the people supporting and opposed to the landfill scheme. After the role play, have a council vote of all students in the class to determine what action will be taken.

4. Have a garbage awareness week in your school. With classmates, pick up litter you find on the school property for a five-day period. Display the garbage collection for other students in the school to view. Design posters that suggest ways of decreasing the amount of garbage produced and encourage students to reduce waste. Include the posters with the garbage display.

5. Plan to achieve a "zero garbage" day. For one day, find ways to recycle materials that you might otherwise throw away. Some suggestions for achieving this goal are the following:
   - Use both sides of all papers and recycle what you don't want to keep.
   - Make sure recycling boxes are handy for home and school use.
   - Set up a composter for use at school and home.

   Write a report about the experience and share it with classmates.

Controversy Corner

Scientific Perspectives on the Greenhouse Effect

Robert Jastrow and William Nierenberg

The temperature of the earth's surface apparently has increased by 0.5°C over the last 100 years. We judge this temperature increase to be real, although its existence has been disputed by some experts.

How reliable is the 0.5°C warming as an indicator of the full greenhouse effect projected for the next century? First, most of the observed rise of 0.5°C occurred in the first 50 years, from 1880 to 1930. But less than a third of the total carbon dioxide increase occurred in that early period. Although greenhouse calculations explain the total increase in global temperature up to 1980, it is not possible for the greenhouse effect to explain the rapid rise in temperature between 1880 and 1930.

Second, from the 1940s to the 1970s, while greenhouse gases continued to build up in the atmosphere, the observed temperatures *decreased* substantially. The decrease was large enough to have a significant agricultural impact on Northern Europe. No sign of this drop in temperature from the 1940s to 1970s appears in the greenhouse forecast for the same period.

The fall in temperature between 1940 and 1970 is particularly difficult to explain as a greenhouse phenomenon, because this entire period was one of strong economic growth and increasing emission of greenhouse gases, and should have been a period of accelerating temperature rise. Even if allowance is made for a delayed response to the increase in the greenhouse gases, the 1940–1970 period should have been one of increasing temperatures—provided the greenhouse effect was actually the main driver of climate change in that period.

These departures from the calculated greenhouse temperature curve suggest that other forces besides the greenhouse effect have been influencing the earth's climate in recent decades. What forces could be changing global temperatures?

Volcanic eruptions are one possibility because they create a layer of particles that reduces the transparency of the atmosphere. Thus, by screening the earth from the sun, volcanoes have a cooling effect. In fact, volcanoes have been suggested as the cause of the substantial temperature drop between 1940 and 1970. However, the observations of the transparency of the atmosphere, which reflect the occurrence of volcanic eruptions, indicate no appreciable reduction in transparency in the 1940–1970 period. Volcanoes influence the climate at times, but cannot account for the observed temperature decrease between 1940 and 1970.

Another possible explanation for the temperature changes in the last 100 years is the natural variability of the earth's climate—changes in climate that occur without any obvious change, i.e., no change in carbon dioxide, volcanic eruptions, or any other factor in climate change. Dr. James Hansen of NASA did a trial 100-year computer run that revealed a substantial natural variability of climate. He found it is possible for the earth's temperature to change by as much as 0.4°C over 25 years as a result of natural climate variability—nearly enough to account for the observed 0.5°C change over the last 100 years.

Finally, satellite measurements show that the sun's brightness can change over time. The measured change was only 0.1%, but astronomical measurements on other stars identical to the sun show changes of up to 0.4% over a period of years—big enough, if they occurred on the sun, to account for the entire 0.5°C temperature increase observed on the earth in the last 100 years.

Evidence in support of solar variability as a significant factor is provided by the accompanying charts, which reveal that the changes in the earth's temperature have followed changes in solar activity over the last 100 years. The charts show that when solar activity increased from the 1880s to the 1940s, global temperatures increased; when solar activity declined from the

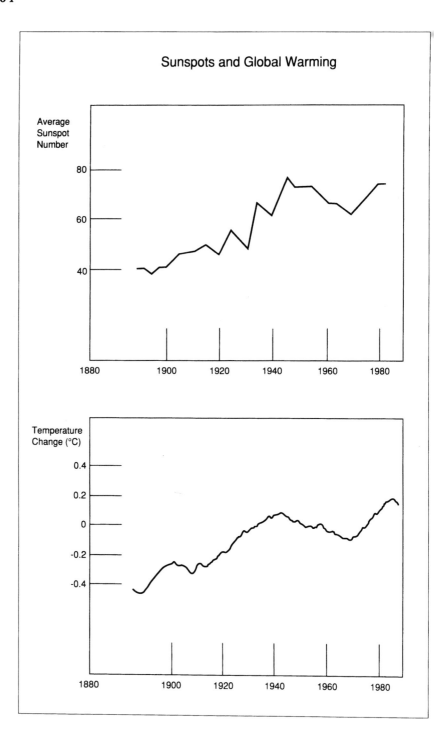

1940s to the 1960s, temperatures also declined; when solar activity and sunspot numbers reversed and started to move up again in the 1970s and 1980s, temperature did the same.

These correlations seem to explain the features that are so puzzling when scientists try to interpret the observed temperatures as a consequence of the greenhouse effect.

The effect of the wild cards introduced into the greenhouse studies by natural and solar variability is that no conclusion about the magnitude of the greenhouse effect into the next century can be drawn from the 0.5°C warming that has occurred in the last 100 years.

The climate record contains another trend that may be useful in forecasting the climate for the 21st century. According to records for the last 800 years, cold spells have occurred in Northern Europe every few hundred years—in the 13th, 15th, 17th, and 19th centuries. The most famous of these is the Little Ice Age of the 17th century, when Northern European temperatures were about 1°C below today's levels. According to these trends, another cold spell is due in the 21st century, with cooling of as much as 1°C. A greenhouse effect at the lower end of the range of current estimates—1°C or less—would only offset the natural cooling, leaving the world's temperature in the 21st century within a degree or so of its present level.

Activities

1. Research a definition of the greenhouse effect by obtaining information from a library vertical file, a book on ecological problems, or an encyclopedia. Share the definition you find with other members of your class.

2. With a partner, locate the points made in this essay that argue against the theory that the world is facing a problem from the greenhouse effect.

3. Find an article that argues that the greenhouse effect and global warming are a real threat to our future. Write an essay explaining which argument you find more persuasive and why you find it so.

4. With a partner, list five environmental problems. For each one, identify a person, group of people, or organization that would benefit if it could be established that no such problem exists.

5. Debate the following: Be it resolved that public concern about the greenhouse effect is exaggerated.

Planting the Seeds of a New Tomorrow

Amy Willard Cross

ow that environmental inanities such as biodegradable diapers and CFC-free aerosol cans fill store shelves and landfills, green consuming is getting a bad name.

But green consuming is *not* about being suckered into biodegradable disposable bags and unleaded gasoline. It is about trying to live privileged, western, twentieth-century lives in an environmentally and socially responsible manner.

Of course, a consuming society dirtied up the planet in the first place, and no amount of politically correct shopping will reverse that. Still, it plays an important role in cleaning up this mess. As environmentalists point out, government and industry lag behind the public when it comes to action. Any significant changes—such as rejecting styrofoam—have been instigated by consumers and public concern.

Obviously, green consuming's primary message is to industry. By boycotts and informed shopping, consumers tell companies what they want. Call it pocket-book voting. It works. Bernadette Vallely of the Women's Environmental Network in Britain reports that a 15 per cent shift in sales gets a product pulled off the shelves. She knows: her campaign generated public outrage at bleaching processes used in sanitary products and diapers and got results. Product changes show just how potent the voices of green consumers can be.

By green consuming, people also demonstrate that a market exists. Kind of a volunteer test market. Hard-core environmentalists first hunted down compact fluorescent bulbs, and now Home Hardware and Canadian Tire catalogues list them. Ontario Hydro is offering a rebate to customers using the super-efficient bulbs. Green consuming trickles up.

Beside using their economic voices, green consumers conduct grass-roots educational campaigns very subtly. Just by going about their lives greenly, they reach an audience that shuns papers and turns the dial during environmental specials. Although the *Canadian Green Consumer Guide* has sold nearly 175,000 copies, the sad fact remains that millions of people commute in automobiles every day and supermarkets sell mostly imported sprayed vegetables. For an environmental evangelist, there's still lots of work to do.

How do green consumers set an example for fellow citizens? At laundromats, they bring soap flakes and powder, explaining to the launderer how ingredients in commercial detergents harm the once great lakes. Lakes where his or her children might one day fish. In their backyard, green consumers compost and grow vegetables without pesticides.

Although launderers and neighbors may shake their heads at such eccentricities, maybe, just maybe, they'll think about it for a minute. Small as it is, each contact lights a little fire. Most will be put out by the winds of laziness or the rains of not giving a damn, but others will ignite.

As usual, children are especially inflammatory. One green 5-year-old made her mother stop shampooing in lakes, buy string bags and reduce short car trips.

Green consumers act as role models. When people go to the trouble of renting glass containers rather than buying plastic, they demonstrate how to live more ecologically to their friends and colleagues. As does serving organically raised meat from a small local farm. Or travelling by train rather than car. Eventually, those role models become unofficial experts. They're asked how to kill bugs naturally or where to buy stuff like plant-based paints. They spread the word.

Although criticized for concentrating on superficial issues—packaging, recycling, household cleaners, composting—green consuming brings the bigger picture into focus. Raising environmental consciousness yields practical effects. Green consuming fosters action and thought—and travels deeper into society.

Once alerted to problems by green consuming, some people who started shopping for a better world now fight for it. Green consumers volunteer at environmental groups, write letters to MPs and lobby in their community.

And after recycling at home, people are cleaning up their businesses by taking green consuming into the marketplace. A Toronto entrepreneur has just come out with *The Green Business Suppliers Guide*. At publisher Lester & Orpen Dennys, a green staffer recycles laser printing toner cartridges and has instituted a strict policy of recycling old manuscripts. The Guelph Board of Education is considering using plant-based non-synthetic paints. And after years of living with this zealously green consumer, my husband was inspired to import and incorporate emission-free canola oil into hydraulic machinery. Clearly, micro-environmentalism leads to macro-environmentalism.

We can only hope that green consumerism continues to spread until every last person shops for a better world. Fights for it. And demands a better, greener life from government and business.

Activities

1. With a partner, identify the author's purpose for writing this essay. Evaluate how effectively the article achieves this purpose.

2. In your journal, list the green products mentioned in the article that are used or have been used in your home. Complete your entry with an evaluation of how green your family is. Indicate what further steps you think your family should take to help save our environment.

3. In a group of three, make a list of five green products available at your local supermarket or another grocery store. Beside each item, indicate whether your group feels it has made a major impact, a minor impact, or no impact at all on the environmental problems facing our world. Compare your list with that of another group.

4. Find an advertisement for a green product. Cut it out and paste it on a sheet of paper. Below the advertisement explain why you would or would not buy this product.

5. Research an article that disputes the effectiveness of a green product or green products in general. Write a summary of the argument presented against the product(s) and explain whether you agree or disagree with the argument. Share your summary and opinion with classmates.

End of Unit Activities

1. Find an article on an environmental problem that includes a photograph. Using a copy of that photograph, prepare a poster that explains the environmental problem represented in it.

2. Find or create three or four cartoons on environmental issues and place them in a scrapbook. Beneath each cartoon write a sentence that identifies the environmental problem being addressed. Prepare a written introduction for your collection and share the book with your classmates.

3. Select a country and identify an environmental problem or issue it faces. You might begin by checking a data base such as the CBCA (Canadian Business and Current Affairs). Write a report on the problem or issue and share it with classmates.

4. Debate one of the following. Research may be necessary.
   - Be it resolved that disposable diapers should be banned.
   - Be it resolved that the cost of water, electricity, and all fuels used for transportation or heating should be increased by 100 per cent to encourage responsible consumption of resources.
   - Be it resolved that all shipping of crude oil be prohibited by international law.
   - Be it resolved that Canada has the right to pressure Brazil about destroying rain forests to improve the standard of living in Brazil.

5. Write an essay on one of the following topics. Research may be necessary.
   - Why I think the planet Earth will survive.
   - You can't have a good life without pollution.
   - It is time for a radical shift in our life style in order to save the planet.
   - The environmental problem that most concerns me is....

Canada's Challenge

What I love about Canada is its civility. There's always a willingness to talk things out—with reasonable politeness.

JANE JACOBS,
URBANOLOGIST

The twentieth century shall be the century of Canada and of Canadian development. For the next seventy-five years, Canada shall be the star towards which all people who love freedom and progress shall come.

SIR WILFRID LAURIER,
PRIME MINISTER OF CANADA, 1896–1911

When they said Canada, I thought it would be in the mountains somewhere.

MARILYN MONROE,
ACTOR

Canadians are no longer not-Americans. We have evolved into a people who are as fully North Americans as are Americans and yet who, because of our political culture, are now a quite distinct kind of North American... Here, two nations have evolved that are utterly alike in almost all of their externals and yet are utterly unalike in their political cultures so that they are as distinct from each other as the Germans from the French.

RICHARD GWYN,
POLITICAL COMMENTATOR

This Vast Land That Shapes Us

Peter C. Newman

anada's least disputable characteristic is size, and my favourite illustration of just how considerable a hunk of geography we occupy is the argument used a few years ago by Pte. Justin Dwyer, stationed with the 2nd Canadian Infantry Brigade near Soest in West Germany, objecting to a transfer to a Canadian army camp at Jericho Beach in British Columbia. He lodged an official complaint, pointing out that the move meant he would be 5,627 kilometres away from his family home at Grand Falls, Nfld., 804 kilometres farther than his NATO service in Germany.

That small example shows vividly the size of this country, and it is our outrageous dimensions that give shape and reason to our identity as Canadians. A West German ambassador in Ottawa once concluded, "I have a country; you have a continent." He was right. Canada laid over a map of Europe would reach from the west coast of Ireland and stretch deep into Asia, east of the Ural Mountains into the heart of the Soviet Union. Ottawa would be located roughly at Kiev, the capital of the Ukraine. It takes six time zones to accommodate Canada's vast expanse, so that when it's 4:30 in the afternoon in Newfoundland, clocks are chiming high noon across the Yukon.

Canada also happens to be the world's most awkwardly designed country. The unwieldy dispersal of our population decides the nature of Canadian life; it affects everything we do in that we have to deal with small numbers of people over enormous distances. The ratio of transportation costs to eventual market price is complex enough to deal with in terms of commodities, but it is very much more difficult for transmitting ideas, culture and emotions from east to west, from

north to even more north, and back again. There is so much
more to geography than space. Marshall McLuhan was correct
when he postulated Canadians' unique relationship with nature:
"We go outside to be alone, and we go inside to be with
people—a pattern that is antithetic not only to Europeans, but
to all other cultures."

That link to the outdoors is reflected not only in our psyches
but our looks. Canadian historian William Kilbourn once
observed, "Outnumbered by the trees and unable to lick them, a
lot of Canadians look as though they joined them—having gone
all faceless or a bit pulp-and-papery, and mournful as the
evening jackpine round the edges of the voice, as if something
long lost and dear were being endlessly regretted." When Dale
Benson, location manager for the movie sequel *Rocky IV*, was
asked why he chose to shoot it in Vancouver, his down-to-earth
reply was that he had picked British Columbians to portray
rugged Soviet citizens watching Sylvester Stallone beating their
hero to a pulp because "Californians look too pretty. You people
look like you've really lived".

It is the streak of nordicity in our national character that
makes us look that way. Territorial integrity (holding on to our
turf, that is) remains our strongest sustaining myth. We happily
give away our energy resources and minerals at rock-bottom
prices, and we sell to foreign investors the most profitable parts
of our secondary manufacturing sector. But let a Yank demand
one drop of our water or sail through the Northwest Passage,
and we respond with outrage. That's why arctic sovereignty,
fishing rights and acid rain (or, for that matter, Quebec
separatism, which is perceived by most English-Canadians as a
threat to the physical continuity of our reach from sea to sea)
have become such hot issues.

It sometimes seems that despite our 122 years of history as a
nation, we are barely a country at all. Yet we have performed
miracles to get as far as we have. To carve even that sliver out of
the wilderness which we now occupy has been an epic of
Homeric proportions, a silent battle against the cold and the
wind and the rocks. Canada is larger than China, with a population smaller than Ethiopia's. Yet less than seven percent of
Canada's landscape is actually settled, and something like three-

quarters of Canada's population is squeezed into less than one
percent of the country's land area—nearly all of it hugging
the United States border. Of our 125 cities, 102 are within
300 kilometres of the American boundary. Most of our
hinterland broods silent and inaccessible, an empty land filled
with wonders.

Because of such population concentrations, there is a curious skew in the way Canada is perceived both by strangers and Canadians. Since exploration and development unyieldingly followed an east-west progression, the centre of the country is usually thought to be located around Winnipeg. In fact, Canada's exact middle is at Baker Lake, an old Hudson's Bay

Company trading post at the head of Chesterfield Inlet, off Hudson Bay.

Apart from our elephantine geography, a favourite rationalization for Canadians' sense of identity is our climate: six months of winter followed by six months of bad sledding. It really does get cold—even in our large cities. Regina has recorded temperatures of -50°C, and temperate Vancouver once hit -20°C. Only the Mongolian capital city of Ulaanbaatar is colder as a capital than Ottawa.

The land's moods, seasons and weathers are the chronometers by which we measure our lives. There is nothing benign about the Canadian landscape, and the epic of civilizing its contours was mostly about hard lives and the anguish of pioneering families discovering themselves and each other too little and too late. Yet it is the land that anchors our sense of who we really are.

"There would be nothing distinctive in Canadian culture at all," says the greatest of our literary critics, Northrop Frye, "if there were not some feeling for the immense searching distance, with the lines of communication extended to the absolute limit, which is a primary geographical fact about Canada and has no real counterpart elsewhere. Everywhere we turn in Canadian literature and painting, we are haunted by the natural world, and even the most sophisticated Canadian artists can hardly keep something very primitive and archaic out of their imaginations."

Given that mystical relationship to the land, it remains one of the great ironies of Canadian topography that an astonishing 37 percent of our Class One agricultural land (on which you can grow almost anything) lies within sight of the top of Toronto's CN Tower—and that so little of that rich loam is still being cultivated or ever can be again.

Perhaps our most powerful geographic feature is the St. Lawrence River, every inch of it, in Hugh MacLennan's magnificent phrase, "measured and brooded over by notaries and blessed by priests". It provides the great Canadian metaphor, defining the emotional difference between arriving on our shores and arriving on the American eastern seaboard, where you step from the wharf directly into the social and commercial heart of that country. "One enters Canada,"

Northrop Frye has written, "through the Strait of Belle Isle into the Gulf of St. Lawrence, where five Canadian provinces surround us, with enormous islands and glimpses of a mysterious mainland in the distance, but in the foreground only sea and sky. Then we go up the waterway of the St. Lawrence, which in itself is only the end of a chain of rivers and lakes that starts in the Rockies.... To enter the United States is a matter of crossing an ocean; to enter Canada is a matter of being silently swallowed by an alien continent."

That 1,200-kilometre journey up the St. Lawrence, so quickly and blithely bypassed by the airlines, ought to be a requirement of Canadian citizenship. It was from the quays along this shoreline that the voyageurs set off along the rippling, rugged rivers that cleave the hinterland. They were in the service of the fur trade, the commerce that first gave substance to the notion of Canada as a transcontinental state. They crossed the Prairies and later the Rockies, claimed the watersheds of the Mississippi and Columbia, and fanned up into the subarctic. They rode the great Churchill River, which roared down to Hudson Bay from the divide at Lac La Loche, site of the infamous Methy Portage, the longest and toughest on the trade routes. Conquering its 20-kilometre trail by climbing a 180-metre elevation under 40-kilogram packs of freight and furs earned voyageurs the ultimate badge of courage. After crossing this formidable rampart, the canoes were in Athabasca Country, whose gloomy forests eventually yielded the world's most prodigious fur catch.

The impact of these transcontinental trading routes was pervasive enough to work the magic that helped save Western Canada from being absorbed into the United States. Holding the land claimed through right of exploration, and later by occupation of the Hudson's Bay and North West companies, was a close call, but it was the scattering of those puny fur-trading outposts that held the line.

One of the essential differences between the geographies of Canada and the United States is that American rivers, such as the Mississippi and Missouri, run across populated basins, giving focus and direction to the communities of their shores. With such exceptions as the St. Lawrence and the Fraser, most of our major rivers run northward, unwatched and unknown. Few Canadians have ever or will ever see the country's longest river, the mighty Mackenzie, whose drainage basin ranks next in size only to the Amazon and Mississippi.

Our image of ourselves is based largely on the contours and colours of our North. It was into our mysterious attic that the Group of Seven painters journeyed most frequently to find their subjects and inspiration. Inventing new techniques to capture the breathtaking magnitude of what they saw, they broke with European schools of painting to refine their exploding vision and put it to canvas. "We came to know that it is only through the deep and vital experience of its total environment that a people identifies itself with its land and gradually a deep and satisfying awareness develops," Lawren Harris reminisced after one northern journey. "We were convinced that no virile people could remain subservient to, and dependent upon, the creations in art of other peoples.... To us there was also the strange brooding sense of nature fostering a new race and a new age."

While no single factor forms a nation's character, winter's dominance, and the North that symbolizes it, rank among Canada's most potent influences. "I've always felt that in Canadians' novels the geography, nature, is not a background, it's a character, as it is in Russia," Canadian novelist John Ralston Saul once explained. "Canadian fiction is much more like Russian fiction than it is like American or English or French."

To most Canadians, North is less a place than a direction— the ultimate reflection of how we view ourselves in relation to the land we call home. "When we face south," contends novelist Margaret Atwood, "our conscious mind may be directed towards crowds, bright lights, some Hollywood version of fame and fortune—but the North is at the back of our minds, always. There's something, not someone, looking over our shoulders; there's a chill at the nape of the neck. The North focuses our anxieties. Turning to face north, we enter our own unconscious. Always, in retrospect, the journey north has the quality of dreams."

Most city dwellers, especially in Central Canada, seldom travel any farther northward than their summer cottages. Yet we are all marked by the wild. As historian W. L. Morton pointed out, "Because of our origin in the northern frontier, Canadian life to this day is marked by a northern quality. The line which marks the frontier from the farmstead, the wilderness from the baseland, the hinterland from the metropolis, runs through every Canadian psyche."

Morton was right. Even in contemporary and highly urbanized Canada, our landscape is our lifeblood. Being Canadian means paying heed to the country's seasonal rhythms, turning our inner ear to the land's music. "From the land," decreed historian A.R.M. Lower, "must come the soul of Canada."

Activities

1. With a partner, select one statement in the essay that you agree with and one that you don't agree with. Be prepared to explain to the class your choices and the basis for your agreement or disagreement.

2. In your own words, write the thesis that Peter Newman proposes in this essay. Identify what you consider to be the strongest and weakest arguments that he uses to support his thesis. Explain what further information you might need to be convinced.

3. Working with a partner, locate on a map of Canada some of the places or geographical phenomena mentioned in the essay. Based on your observations, decide whether Peter Newman's main thesis in the essay is valid.

4. Select one of the people quoted in the essay and find information about the person in *The Canadian Encyclopedia*. Make a report to your classmates about the individual and the contribution he or she made to our country.

5. In a journal entry, write what you think is the biggest challenge facing Canada today. Explain the reasons for your choice.

6. Have each member of the class write an ending to the sentence "Canada is..." Arrange the completed sentences in a bulletin board display about the country.

The Mysterious North

Pierre Berton

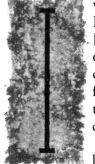 was brought up in a small frame cottage in Dawson City, where the walls were a foot [30 cm] thick and filled with sawdust to keep out the cold, where a pot of dog food—rice and caribou meat—bubbled perpetually over a wood fire, and where the water was brought around to the door in icicle-draped buckets at twenty-five cents a pail.

Our home lay nestled against the low bench-land that skirts the swampy flats beside the gray Yukon River. Behind us rose the black bulk of the hills, clothed in spruce and birch and poplar. Behind those hills lay other hills, and when you climbed to the top of the farthest hills, there were yet more hills stretching endlessly into the north. If a man wanted to walk in a straight line due north he could cross those hills for four hundred miles [640 km] until he reached the edge of the Arctic sea, and he would come upon no trace of human life.

I have never quite been able to escape the memory of those lonely hills. In the winter nights, when the roar of the river was hushed by a mantle of ice, when the frost-racked timbers cracked like pistol-shots in the cold, when the ghostly bars of the northern lights shifted across the black sky, we would sometimes hear the chill call of the wolf, drifting down from the wilderness behind us. It is an eerie sound, plaintive, mournful, mysterious. The wolf is like the husky and the malemute: his vocal cords are so constructed that he cannot bark, but only howl across the endless hills. If the north has a theme song, it is this haunting cry, which seems to echo all the loneliness and the wonder of the land at the top of the continent.

When I was a small boy, it used to fascinate and terrify me, perhaps because in all my years in the north I never actually saw a wolf alive. To me he was only a footprint in the snow and a sound in the night, an unseen creature who lurked in the shadow of the nameless hills.

For eleven childhood winters I heard the cry of the wolf, and then I left the country with no intention of returning. But the north has dogged my footsteps and I have never quite been quit of it. Within five years I was back again on the aspen-covered slopes of the Klondike, working with a pick and shovel in a gold camp. I spent three summers at it and then, when war broke out, I left it again, believing that this was the end. It was only the beginning: since those days in the Yukon I have crisscrossed the north from the Alaska border to the tip of Baffin Island, from Churchill on Hudson Bay to Coppermine on the Arctic coast. I have eaten moose steak on the Peace River, buffalo meat in Fort Smith, Arctic grayling in Whitehorse, and reindeer burgers in Aklavik. I have driven the Alaska Highway in a Ford, landed in Headless Valley in a Junkers, crossed Great Slave Lake in a tugboat, and chugged into the heart of Labrador on an ore train...

The more I see of the country, the less I feel I know about it. There is a saying that after five years in the north every man is an expert; after ten years, a novice. No man can hope or expect to absorb it all in a lifetime, and fifteen generations of explorers, whalers, fur traders, missionaries, scientists, policemen, trappers, prospectors, adventurers, and tourists have failed to solve all its riddles. To me, as to most northerners, the country is still an unknown quantity, as elusive as the wolf, howling just beyond the rim of the hills. Perhaps that is why it holds its fascination....

Activities

1. With a partner, identify five vivid memories that Pierre Berton reveals about his youth in the Klondike. For each memory, explain what words in the description indicate how he feels about the memory.

2. Many authors have written essays describing their search for Canada's identity as a nation. After rereading the last paragraph of this essay, discuss in a group of four the extent to which Pierre Berton's comments on the Klondike apply to Canada as a whole. Be prepared to report on your group's observations to the class.

3. In a journal entry, describe some aspect of your youth that either delights or terrifies you and that will probably always remain with you.

4. With a partner, compare Pierre Berton's memories of his childhood with those of Margaret Laurence in her essay "A Place to Stand On" (p. 35). Discuss some of the similarities and differences in their recollections. Write a report that clearly describes the similarities and differences that you found.

The Fragile State of the Francosaskois

Matthew Fisher

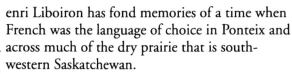enri Liboiron has fond memories of a time when French was the language of choice in Ponteix and across much of the dry prairie that is south-western Saskatchewan.

The retired wheat farmer recalled that, during the Depression, his father learned English from the Eaton's catalogue and that every mass, marriage and burial service was conducted in French.

The language was important enough that the town's first grocer, Theodore Kouri, taught himself French in order to do business.

So when Mr. Liboiron got together with 200 of his relatives for a family reunion this summer [1990], he was saddened that in order to efficiently organize a group photograph he had to speak almost entirely in English.

After the photo session, the 61-year-old bachelor quietly switched to Quebec-style French to lament the fragile state of his mother tongue in Saskatchewan.

"The French have always been the majority around Ponteix since 1908, but the language has been on the slide for years," said Mr. Liboiron, who described himself as an amateur anthropologist. "With the Meech Lake mess, it will get even worse. The assimilation rate is already really fantastic. It looks like we'll disappear here within 20 years."

Overhearing the conversation, one of Mr. Liboiron's French-speaking relatives, Viateur Chabot, came over to offer an even more pessimistic assessment.

"It would be so damn nice to have both languages, but all this fighting about Meech Lake has killed it," Mr. Chabot, 54, said. "It has taken away all our tolerance.

"It's like kids who scream: 'That's my toy.' The result is that the French outside Quebec are going down the tubes. It's impossible to be French anywhere else."

It did not seem that way when eight families of Liboirons struck out for Saskatchewan from Quebec before the First World War to test a federal promise of cheap, arable land. The Liboirons were joined in opening up the West by thousands of like-minded French-speaking homesteaders from Quebec, France and Belgium and franco-Americans from Quebec who came out West after first trying their luck in New England, Minnesota and North Dakota.

With the help and encouragement of Grey Nuns and Oblate priests, the land-hungry, would-be farmers broke tens of thousands of hectares of land from southern Manitoba to northwestern Alberta. In so doing, they established more than 70 French-speaking communities, as well as many of the first schools and hospitals in western Canada.

To thank God for their good fortune, the colonists built magnificent churches and convents like those along the St. Lawrence River. The huge buildings can still be seen from kilometres away, lonely sentinels towering over prairie towns such as Ponteix, Gravelbourg and Lafleche. Nearby are graveyards filled with headstones and statues honoring priests and pioneers with old French names such as Elphège, Ovide and Ovila.

"When I was young, everyone here was French and everyone was Catholic. Everyone was me," Mr. Liboiron said. "That's why when I started school it was a revelation to me to discover that the English language existed."

There are about 23,000 francosaskois today. They live mostly near Prince Albert and North Battleford in central Saskatchewan and in communities near the Montana border such as Ponteix, Gravelbourg, Cadillac and Willow Bunch, where Jeanne Sauvé, the former Governor-General, was born.

Since the Roman Catholic Church established the bishop's residence and a college at Gravelbourg, which is about an hour's drive northeast of Ponteix, it has always been viewed as the centre of French life in Saskatchewan. But with an influx of thousands of German immigrants to Gravelbourg after the Second World War, the French are a rapidly diminishing minority there.

Its hold in tiny Ponteix is precarious, but the French language may be stronger here than anywhere else in Saskatchewan today. As elsewhere on the Prairies, years of drought and depressed wheat prices have caused hundreds of Ponteix's children to leave for jobs in Alberta, Ontario and Quebec. But the economy is so bad that few non-francophones have moved in.

Therefore, Ponteix's 80:20 ratio of French to English has been preserved. About 450 of the village's 600 remaining residents are of French descent, although only a couple of hundred of them use the language regularly.

In the early years, when the CPR was the only way in or out of town, the French thrived in isolation. But as Saskatchewan established what has become one of the most comprehensive road networks in Canada, the province's sleepy French towns became exposed to more and more English influences. When television finally came in the early sixties, assimilation progressed rapidly.

After a marvellous beginning, being a francophone in Saskatchewan began to become politically difficult in the early thirties when premier James Anderson restricted French-language schooling to a maximum of one hour a day. When French residents of Ponteix protested, the Ku Klux Klan, which was quite active in the province then, burned a cross in front of the school and put up the Union Jack and a picture of the British King.

"What rights can we lose? What rights do we have?" asked Béatrice Sylvain, who was a student during those turbulent times.

"The only way I kept the language is that my parents absolutely insisted upon it at home," Ms. Sylvain, who now lives in Le Manoir retirement home, said.

Shaking his head slowly, Mr. Liboiron, who received a little schooling in French before the law was changed, said: "Anderson just hated us. He wanted to wipe us out and getting at us through the schools was the best way."

Two of those continuing the seemingly interminable struggle for the right to be educated in French in Saskatchewan today are Denis and Doris Roberge. Their four children are 12th generation French-Canadians. They are enrolled in a French immersion program and there is talk of trying to get a full-fledged French school.

The battle is now over whether the withering rural tax base can support two levels of French schooling.

"We fought for 10 years to get French immersion, but it was incredibly difficult," said Mr. Roberge, whose own French is rougher than that of his children.

"You wouldn't believe it, but we were called separatists and all kinds of things," the 34-year old farmer and part-time miner said. "There were some English against it, but it was mostly the French who objected. You see, they'd already lost the language."

Relations may be better now between francophone loyalists and the English and their improbable allies, the assimilated French, but controversies still come up from time to time. For example, earlier this year, some residents of Gravelbourg complained loudly when the French college there set aside an hour a week of public swimming exclusively for francophone families. The critics said this was unfair to non-francophone residents although the pool, which is jointly operated by the school and the town, is otherwise open to all residents except when being used by the college.

Theodore Kouri said it was easy to exaggerate linguistic and cultural tensions. But a moment later the retired shopkeeper mentioned that he was annoyed that the local French society office carried a large fleur-de-lis and a small maple leaf on the sign over its front door.

Mr. Kouri moved to Ponteix with his family in the thirties and was mayor of the community for 27 years. The pensioner said he had a few neighbors who complained bitterly about the state of French in Saskatchewan.

"But these same people don't care enough about their language to speak it with their grandchildren," he said. "Now, whose fault is that?"

One of those who was not very sympathetic about the need to fight for French-language rights is Lucille Bertrand. She was back home for the Bertrand family reunion after many years in Edmonton.

"I have difficulty understanding what the true issue is," Mrs. Morden said. "Whether we are French, Germans, Ukrainian or

Scottish doesn't make any difference. We should all have our cultures, but there is no need to make a ruckus about it. We're too far away from Quebec to have French pushed down our throats."

Clara Provencal, a pensioner who has lived in the area her whole life, said she was untroubled by the decreasing use of French.

Looking bemused that anyone should be interested in this, Ms. Provencal asked in French: "Why be bothered if your kids speak English?"

Henri Liboiron said such attitudes exasperated him.

"Sure some of their kids speak English and I ask myself why," Mr. Liboiron said, mopping his heavily furrowed brow with his baseball cap. "The reason is that after all these years they've grown sick of fighting.

"They say we speak lousy French, but I can read Molière. I'm not a linguist. I'm a farmer. But I don't understand how some people think that if Canada speaks only one language we will have a better world."

Activities

1. In a journal entry, indicate whether you favour or oppose small towns such as Ponteix maintaining a special language and cultural identity. If your own community has a particular cultural identity, explain your ideas about preserving it.

2. Divide the class into twelve groups and assign each group a province or territory of Canada. Research and prepare a class radio documentary based on your findings about the following topics:
   - cities and towns in the area with French names
   - cities and towns with other European or native names
   - settlement patterns that the names suggest

3. Research and prepare a report about French-English relations in Canada on one of the following topics:
   - early French and English settlements in Upper and Lower Canada
   - French language and cultural rights in the British North America Act
   - Louis Riel
   - the Parti Quebecois
   - Canada's bilingual and bicultural policies today
   - the Meech Lake Accord

4. In a group of three, list ways in which you or young people you know participate in activities related to preserving cultural heritage. Write a journal entry explaining how important your cultural heritage is to you.

Pride and Prejudice

Pete McMartin

In the spring of 1990, the Vancouver *Sun* newspaper sent reporter Pete McMartin to Quebec for two weeks to travel by car around the province. The following essay gives his personal impressions of the people and places he encountered.

In Rimouski, which is a bastion of francophone pride, there is a McDonald's. The true lingua franca of the world is not English, it is "le Big Mac," and whenever I felt hungry enough, but too exhausted to wrestle with an all-French menu, I looked for the golden arches.

So I'm in Rimouski. I decided to try out my high school French. It was lunch hour, extremely busy. Stepping up to the counter, and as tentative as a cat crossing water, I said to the server behind the counter, "Je desire un Big Mac et frites, s'il vous plait." The girl's face fell. She was agog. She handed me the food and watched me go.

It wasn't until a week and a half later that I found out what I had said. A photographer from the Montreal *Gazette*, laughing at my Rimouski encounter, explained the nuances of Quebec French to me. Yes, "je desire" meant "I want," but she said I might have been better to say "je voudrais"—"I would like." "Je desire"—in Quebec—usually carried an urgent emotional or physical inference, such as "Je desire to rip your clothes off and make you my love slave." I hadn't ordered hamburger; I had asked to have carnal relations with it. Imagine what the French of Rimouski think of us English.

I don't want to make too big a metaphor out of this; after all, the English and French have been misunderstanding each other for centuries. And it's a pity, because underneath we are all the same. A Big Mac is un Big Mac, no matter how you say it.

But this was the idea: I was to try and get by in Quebec without speaking French. It was to be a test of the Quebeckers' tolerance. I was to be a stranger in a strange land.

And this, too: I was not to speak to any politicians, premiers, lobbyists, self-appointed guardians of the faith. I was to talk to people. People like you, reader, who in the privacy of their dens and with a beer in their hands, mutter, "What in hell do those English want? They're tearing this country apart."

Before I left, I wasn't convinced they were there. All I knew of Quebec was what I had heard. Apocryphal stories of Quebec abound. They all wear berets, smoke Gauloises, and curse "les maudits anglais" between slurps of bad French wine. They will refuse to speak English to you. The waiters are rude. They hate Canada because they lost on the Plains of Abraham.

And, of course, I didn't find a single person like that.

"On a political level or a collective level," said David Johnston, a Montreal *Gazette* reporter who has travelled extensively in Quebec, "the French can be a pain in the ass. But on an individual level, the opposite is the case. What many people don't know, on an individual level, the Quebec people are incredibly generous."

I found a thousand small kindnesses. There was the time I got lost in Port Daniel East and I was looking for the municipal hall in Port Daniel West. Port Daniel East is entirely French: Port Daniel West, on the other side of the river valley, is bilingual. Stopping in a shabby Port Daniel East corner store, I tried asking for directions. The woman at the counter couldn't speak a word of English, so we communicated through much hand-waving and what I came to call idiot-speech. I would say very slowly, and loudly enough for the hearing-impaired, "I... AM...LOOKING...FOR...THE...MUNICIPAL...HALL." And I guessed she was saying in French, "I...DON'T... UNDERSTAND...A...WORD... YOU...ARE...SAYING! AND...WHY...ARE...YOU...SHOUTING?"

We were rescued by her husband, who could not speak English either, but who did understand "taxes," "mayor," "place." He drew me a map, and then commanded a young French guy who was unlucky enough to stop by at that moment for cigarettes to drive me to the Port Daniel West municipal hall.

There were the three waitresses at the Dixie Lee take-out restaurant in Bonaventure. The specialty was fried chicken.

The menu, as always, was in French.

"Excusez-moi, mesdames, je suis un journalist au Vancouver et mon francais est très mal. Qu'est-ce que c'est 'poitrine'?"

Any attempt at French in Quebec—any—is universally appreciated, and usually greeted with an insistence that the conversation be conducted in English. The Quebecois do this out of politeness, but also out of their desire, in my experience, anyway, to try out their English. The three waitresses diplomatically assured me I had a wonderful grasp of their language, and then brought out a whole chicken for me.

"Poitrine," one said, and using some tongs as a pointer, pointed to the chicken breast. We ran over the entire anatomy this way, until I had a pretty good idea of what I was ordering. They waved goodbye when I left. It went better than Rimouski.

In St. Joseph-de-Beauce, I met the family who spent 15 minutes on the phone for me looking for the person I was supposed to interview. I was lost, and had arrived on their doorstep on a Sunday unannounced. None of them could speak English. A young son was in the family room playing Nintendo. Another young son was cleaning a rifle. The mother smiled sweetly and insisted I come inside. The father made a dozen phone calls and still didn't find the man I was to interview. Finally, he phoned the one man he knew who could speak English and told him I was coming. He drew a map. The man who spoke English turned out to be a maker of piano sounding boards, and who had just sold four of them to a Vancouver firm. His wife was upset that he was spending his Sunday talking to a reporter from across the country when he had worked all week, but he sat down and talked for a half-hour, anyway.

These are not isolated examples. In my experiences, the equanimity of the Quebecois was universal. Even in the heart of separatist Montreal, on infamous St. Denis Street, I could always be served in English and conduct a conversation in English.

"I think French Canadians are really wounded by what's happened in English Canada," said Lawrence Kootnikoff, a free-lance journalist from Quebec City. Kootnikoff is from White Rock. He went to Quebec with his own preconceived notions of the place, only to find they had little relation to reality.

"I was surprised by it, by English Canada's reaction—the unilingual declarations by municipalities, the Quebec flag-burning, the booing of the national anthem when it was sung in French at the Sky Dome. There were times when I felt so ashamed to be an English Canadian. I don't see the same level of hostility coming from this province.

"Something that really struck me was the gulf between Quebec and the rest of Canada. That's our problem now; the lack of communication."

Kootnikoff experienced what many do who spend time in Quebec: they are struck by the difference between the graciousness of the people and the image that the Quebecois political establishment projects to the rest of Canada.

Said Don MacPherson, political columnist for the Montreal *Gazette*: "If you stopped reading newspapers, you wouldn't realize there was a language conflict in Quebec. There is a tremendous weariness with the idea here. People just want to get on with life. In a column, I described it as a war fought by surrogate warriors so people could get on with their everyday lives. In terms of civility, the people in this province are exceptional.

"For example, Montreal is officially unilingual. But whenever they sing the national anthem, it's always bilingual. Go figure.

"I find," MacPherson said, "people here are more tolerant of cultural and racial differences than the rest of the country. They're certainly no worse."

However, Quebec can give rise to someone like Pierre Peladeau, the newspaper publisher who recently said Jews "took up too much room" in Quebec. MacPherson argues that Peladeau was roundly criticized by all segments of the Quebec establishment and was forced to retract his statement. (He was also denied an honorary degree he was to receive.) MacPherson also cites figures from the B'nai Brith that state the number of anti-semitic incidents in Quebec were, per capita, among the lowest among the Canadian provinces.

But Peladeau exists, and so, among Quebec society, do his ideas. But to use Peladeau as the litmus to judge Quebecois tolerance would be a mistake, just as it would be a mistake to judge Vancouver tolerance over the reaction to the influx of

Hong Kong money. (We have more in common with Quebec than we think.) By and large, people get along in Quebec, just as they do here. The oldest Jewish community in Canada is in the heart of Montreal. So making any generalizations about Quebec, or making any assumptions, is fraught with peril.

I will make one generalization. From what I saw, heard, and read, Quebec—not unlike Canada itself—exists as a duality. This duality contributes to the Quebecois' profound sense of confusion about themselves and their relationship to the rest of Canada. The most vibrantly cultural province exists within the most reactionary. The intellectual community, for example, is revered in Quebec like in no other province, but it can be so maudlinly self-absorbed as to be laughable. One Quebecois intellectual told me there is no such thing as an English Canadian intelligentsia, and that the idea of English Canada itself is an abstraction. The Quebec press rail at English Canada's misinterpretation of Quebec's aspirations, but how many Quebec papers send their reporters to English Canada to see what it is thinking? We're still waiting.

This duality, and enraging self-absorption, give rise to confusion. How does English Canada know what to think of Quebec when Quebec has trouble deciding what it wants for itself?

"My favorite headline of all," said Kootnikoff, "is the headline in *La Presse* (Montreal's big French daily newspaper). It said: '56 per cent of Quebeckers for Sovereignity—53 per cent opposed to Separation.' More Quebeckers see themselves reflected in the uncertainty of that headline than those who believe they should separate and become an independent country. There's a comedian in Quebec, Yvon Duchamp, who had a famous line about what the Quebecois want—'a free and independent Quebec within a strong and united Canada.' "

Eric Desaulniers, a 24-year-old hotel clerk in Rimouski, would like Quebec to separate from Canada, not because he feels hard done by by the English, but because he is tired of paying exorbitant taxes to two governments.

"I think with (former Quebec Premier Rene) Levesque it was revenge. But for me, I just want to go our own way."

Desaulniers would very much like to visit B.C. one day.

But down the road, at the gas station, 28-year-old Claire D'Amboise thinks separatism is crazy. She works the cash register because she couldn't get a job as an interpreter after going to college to study languages. She speaks English and French, and reads Russian, German and Latin.

"I hope they don't separate. I don't know much about politics, but I live here, and a lot of people are out of work and a lot of people rely on unemployment. I understand why they want to do it, because they feel they are going to lose their identity. But I speak English and French, and I haven't lost my identity."

What does she think is the English image of the Quebecois?

"Oh, a big pain somewhere," Claire says. "We're always yelling."

They have no monopoly on that in this nation. If there was one sentiment I came away with from Quebec, it is that too many of the wrong people are doing the yelling—the Nunziatas, the Buchanans, the Peladeaus, the Parizeaus, the pitiful yahoos of the Alliance for the Preservation of English Canada, the religiously blinkered zealots of the Montreal Catholic School Commission—people who, in an effort to reflect their own stature, would have this country become smaller.

I didn't meet anyone like that. All I met were people who went out of their way to make a stranger in a strange land comfortable, whether they could speak my language or not. They make good neighbors.

Activities

1. With a partner, list several reasons the author presents for the gulf that exists between Quebec and the rest of Canada. Add to the list your own ideas based on personal experience, television programs, and reading you have done. Present your list to the class for their comments.

2. Find a piece of information contained in the essay that either surprised you or revealed facts you didn't know. Discuss the material you choose with a partner.

3. In a journal entry, write your thoughts about one of the following topics:
   - why you would or would not like to visit Quebec
   - an experience you had while visiting Quebec or entertaining visitors from Quebec
   - your attitude toward bilingual packaging in all of Canada
   - Quebec remaining as a province of Canada

4. Write a journal entry explaining where you stand on the issue of Quebec sovereignty.

5. Role play a situation in which a unilingual English-speaking Canadian asks a unilingual French-speaking Canadian
   - for directions to the local library,
   - where to buy a newspaper,
   - for a date.

   Perform the role play for others. Use both languages and body language where appropriate.

6. Research a newspaper or magazine article on the separatist movement in Quebec. Present a summary of the information it contains to the class.

A Purple World

Richard Wagamese

aterton Lakes—When the sun sets behind these mountains you can almost see them begin to breath. It's a trick of the light, really, something created by the encroaching purple darkness, distance and an indefinable desire for magic.

The Old Ones believed that this was a strong spirit time. The grandfathers and grandmothers whose spirits reside within these trees, rocks, rivers and mountains would come alive again and around those ancient tribal fires their songs would be sung and the drums would echo the heartbeat of the universe to welcome them.

My *mishomis,* Ojibway for grandfather, described this time and the mountains breathing as the universe giving a collective shrug. It was his way of saying that the earth is alive.

The earth is alive. It was ironic to be perched on a rock at the edge of a small, rushing river in the back country of southern Alberta's most beautiful park, while Environment Week [June 3–9, 1991] rolled into gear across the country. Here, amid the rough and tangle of pristine creation, the thought of a special week designed to focus attention on the earth as a living, breathing entity was an elegant redundancy.

In the Indian way of seeing, the land, and all things that move upon it, is alive and therefore sacred. Humankind's relationship to the earth and its life-forms has always been that of an equal. The honor of one is the honor of all. If you cared enough to consider the guardianship of yourself and your family, it followed that you care enough to consider the guardianship of the earth.

Here, in the gathering darkness, in the middle of what the whiteman so loosely terms *wilderness,* it was good to consider these things.

There was never a term for wilderness in native tongues. Wilderness is a European term that simply means something that can't be controlled. For the Indians there was never any need or desire to control, to fear or to abuse something which you were a part of. There was only a need, and a responsibility, to preserve it. So the destruction of forests, the damming of rivers, the depletion of resources and the extinction of animals has always been mystifying to the aboriginal peoples.

It all comes down to the idea of one heartbeat. A spiritual connectedness to those things that surround us and a realization that the reverse of the honor of one philosophy, logically, is the dishonor of all. This is spiritual, this is truth, this is Indian.

But the establishment of a spiritual connection to the earth isn't enough. It's a good foundation for an individual or a society, but the aboriginal peoples believed that a feeling could only become a belief and a principle if it were acted upon. So it was necessary for every tribal member to practise the idea of guardianship for all things.

Young people were taught the principles of respect and waste management virtually from the moment they could understand. Life was sacred and since all things were seen to be alive, respect meant taking and using only that which was necessary. If a life-form needed to be used, nothing was wasted. There were no land fills in pre-settlement North America.

It was good for me, an urban-based aboriginal person, to remember these things. Life in the city and existence in a cosmopolitan society has a sly way of taking you away from the philosophies and traditions of centuries. It's not long before the frantic sweep of modern living erases the recollections of the wisdom of the Old Ones.

So for me, sitting there watching the world become a purple place was a vital reconnection to the environmental foundations of my people's view of the world.

Walking along the parched bed of a mountain stream made it easy to imagine this place as it must have been two or three hundred years ago—untrammelled and free. These same rocks that have sat untouched for generations have their stories and it's becoming open enough to realize this and to listen for them that instigates the reconnection.

One week devoted to refocusing on environmental concerns isn't enough for anyone. Seven days to be reminded of the fact that the earth is a living, breathing entity won't halt the continued rape and plunder of finite resources; nor will it guarantee a collective mindset geared towards environmental protectionism. But it's a start.

What it takes is a walk upon the land. Learning to see these things that exist here with something other than your eyes. Leaving the material trappings behind awhile and allowing yourself to become a part of the sweep and grandeur of the planet; allowing your heartbeat to echo the universal heartbeat.

When you do that you learn to see the mountains, begin to breathe in the falling darkness. You learn to accept the responsibility that comes with being a part of creation and you begin to understand, as the Old Ones understand, that the honor of one thing is the honor of all.

Activities

1. In a group of three, discuss your responses to the questions below. Be prepared to present the group's ideas to the class.
   - Of what significance is the fact that there is no term for wilderness in native languages?
   - Do you agree that "Life in the city and existence in a cosmopolitan society has a sly way of taking you away from the philosophies and traditions of centuries"? Is this statement true for non-native Canadians?
   - Do you agree that celebrating Environment Week "isn't enough"? Does celebrating Environment Week serve a purpose?

2. Select a sentence from this essay that you think is well phrased. Be prepared to share your example with the class, explaining why you chose it.

3. With a partner,
   - identify the author's purpose for writing this essay,
   - determine whether more factual information would strengthen the essay,
   - describe the kind of information the author presents to develop his point of view.

   Be prepared to report your ideas and observations to the rest of the class.

4. With a partner, list actions people take that reveal a disrespect for the Earth. Using one example, make a poster that draws attention to the action and encourages respect for the environment.

5. As a class, brainstorm examples of environmental issues that native Canadians are addressing today. Your list might include issues such as the preservation of forests and the protection of traditional hunting and fishing grounds. On your own, research the controversy surrounding one of these issues and prepare a report to present to the class.

'I'm Not Racist But...'

Neil Bissoondath

someone recently said that racism is as Canadian as maple syrup. I have no argument with that. History provides us with ample proof. But, for proper perspective, let us remember that it is also as American as apple pie, as French as croissants, as Jamaican as ackee, as Indian as aloo, as Chinese as chow mein, as… Well, there's an entire menu to be written. This is not by way of excusing it. Murder and rape, too, are international, multicultural, innate to the darker side of the human experience. But we must be careful that the inevitable rage evoked does not blind us to the larger context.

The word "racism" is a discomforting one: It is so vulnerable to manipulation. We can, if we so wish, apply it to any incident involving people of different color. And therein lies the danger. During the heat of altercation, we seize, as terms of abuse, on whatever is most obvious about the other person. It is, often, a question of unfortunate convenience. A woman, because of her sex, easily becomes a female dog or an intimate part of her anatomy. A large person might be dubbed "a stupid ox," a small person "a little" whatever. And so a black might become "a nigger," a white "a honky," an Asian "a paki," a Chinese "a chink," an Italian "a wop," and French-Canadian "a frog."

There is nothing pleasant about these terms; they assault every decent sensibility. Even so, I once met someone who, in a stunning surge of naiveté, used them as simple descriptives and not as terms of racial abuse. She was horrified to learn the truth. While this may have been an extreme case, the point is that the use of such patently abusive words may not always indicate racial or cultural distaste. They may indicate ignorance or stupidity or insensitivity, but pure racial hatred—such as the Nazis held for Jews, or the Ku Klux Klan for blacks—is a thankfully rare commodity.

Ignorance, not the wilful kind but that which comes from lack of experience, is often indicated by that wonderful phrase, "I'm not racist but…" I think of the mover, a friendly man, who said, "I'm not racist, but the Chinese are the worst drivers on the road." He was convinced this was so because the shape of their eyes, as far as he could surmise, denied them peripheral vision.

Or the oil company executive, an equally warm and friendly man, who, looking for an apartment in Toronto, rejected buildings with East Indian tenants not because of their race— he was telling me this, after all—but because he was given to understand that cockroaches were symbols of good luck in their culture and that, when they moved into a new home, friends came by with gift-wrapped roaches.

Neither of these men thought of himself as racist, and I believe they were not, deep down. (The oil company executive made it clear he would not hesitate to have me as a neighbor; my East Indian descent was of no consequence to him, my horror of cockroaches was.) Yet their comments, so innocently delivered, would open them to the accusation, justifiably so if this were all one knew about them. But it is a charge which would undoubtedly be wounding to them. It is difficult to recognize one's own misconceptions.

True racism is based, more often than not, on wilful ignorance, and an acceptance of—and comfort with—stereotype. We like to think, in this country, that our multicultural mosaic will help nudge us into a greater openness. But multiculturalism as we know it indulges in stereotype, depends on it for a dash of colour and the flash of dance. It fails to address the most basic questions people have about each other: Do those men doing the Dragon Dance really all belong to secret criminal societies? Do those women dressed in saris really coddle cockroaches for luck? Do those people in dreadlocks all smoke marijuana and live on welfare? Such questions do not seem to be the concern of the government's multicultural programs, superficial and exhibitionistic as they have become.

So the struggle against stereotype, the basis of all racism, becomes a purely personal one. We must beware of the impressions we create. A friend of mine once commented that, from talking to West Indians, she has the impression that their one great cultural contribution to the world is the oft-repeated boast that "We (unlike everyone else) know how to party."

There are dangers, too, in community response. We must be wary of the self-appointed activists who seem to pop up in the media at every given opportunity spouting the rhetoric of retribution, mining distress for personal, political and professional gain. We must be skeptical about those who depend on conflict for their sense of self, the non-whites who need to feel themselves victims of racism, the whites who need to feel themselves purveyors of it. And we must be sure that, in addressing the problem, we do not end up creating it. Does the *Miss Black Canada Beauty Contest* still exist? I hope not. Not only do I find beauty contests offensive, but a racially segregated one even more so. What would the public reaction be, I wonder, if every year CTV broadcast the *Miss White Canada Beauty Pageant?* We give community-service awards only to blacks: Would we be comfortable with such awards only for whites? In Quebec, there are The Association of Black Nurses, The Association of Black Artists, The Congress of Black Jurists. Play tit for tat: The Associations of White Nurses, White Artists, White Jurists: visions of apartheid. Let us be frank, racism for one is racism for others.

Finally, and perhaps most important, let us beware of abusing the word itself.

Activities

1. Select five words in this essay that you feel explain how the author responds to racism. For each word, identify the emotion it suggests to you. Share your list with a partner.

2. With a partner, identify examples that illustrate what the author means by racism based on:
   - ignorance,
   - willful ignorance,
   - pure racial hatred.

   Share your examples with another partnership.

3. In a group of three, read the second to last paragraph of the essay and identify the arguments you might make to support
   - the existence of ethnic clubs and neighbourhoods,
   - awards that recognize members of racial, cultural, or religious groups.

4. In a journal entry,
   a) describe a time when you or someone you know inadvertently said or did something that offended a member of a race, culture, religion, age, or sex different from your own

   OR

   b) describe an example of a situation in which a person was unfairly accused of racism.

5. In a complex society such as ours, race is not the only basis for discrimination. With a partner,
   - identify three groups of people that you feel are discriminated against for reasons other than race,
   - explain the nature of the discrimination involved,
   - consider strategies for overcoming these forms of discrimination.

   Share your ideas and strategies with other partnerships.

6. Read a newspaper or magazine article that identifies discrimination as one of its issues. Write an explanation of the role discrimination plays in the situation that the article describes.

7. Research information about a person from your cultural background who has made a noteworthy contribution to Canadian society (in music, sports, politics, etc.) and prepare a report for the class. If possible, include a photograph of the individual or a video or audio tape about the person as part of the report.

8. Debate the following: Be it resolved that in our multicultural society Christmas should be a personal religious observation, not a national holiday.

Why Canada Has to Beat Its Literacy Problem

June Callwood

arole Boudrias shudders when she remembers the time she almost swallowed Drano because she thought it was Bromo. Even more painful to recall is the time she mistook adult pain-killers for the child-size dose and made her feverish child much sicker.

"When you can't read," she explains, "it's like being in prison. You can't travel very far from where you live because you can't read street signs. You have to shop for food but you don't know what's in most of the packages. You stick to the ones in a glass jar or with a picture on the label. You can't look for bargains because you can't understand a sign that says 'Reduced.' I would ask the clerk where is something and the clerk would say, aisle five. Only I couldn't read aisle five. I'd pretend that I was confused so they'd lead me right to the shelf."

Carole Boudrias is able to read now, at last. She's a 33-year-old single parent who lives with her five children in a handsome townhouse on Toronto's harbourfront and holds a steady job. But her struggle with illiteracy is all too vivid in her memory. "You can't get a job," she says earnestly. "You can't open a bank account. You have to depend on other people. You feel you don't belong. You can't help your children. You can't help yourself."

Six years ago when her oldest child started school, the boy floundered. Because he had been raised in a household without books, print was strange to him. He would point to a word in his reader, that classic, endearingly silly *Dick and Jane*, and ask his mother what it was. She was as baffled as he, so he'd check with his teacher the next day and that evening would proudly read the new word to his mother. She began to absorb the shape of the words he identified. She found she could recognize them even days later.

That was astonishing. As a child she had been labelled mentally retarded and confined to "opportunity classes" where reading wasn't taught. She grew up believing that she wasn't intelligent enough to learn. Nevertheless, she was learning. The vocabulary of words she could read in her son's reader was growing. She began to think maybe the experts were wrong. Then, one miraculous day, she realized she was learning to read even faster than her son was.

"My son was my first teacher," she grins. She had never allowed herself to believe that it was possible that she could learn to read. She hadn't even tried: no one whose life is made up of poverty and failed relationships is ready to take on, voluntarily, the potential for another defeat, another kick in the self-esteem. She hesitated a long time but the evidence was persuasive—she was beginning to read. Her welfare worker had always been kind, so she summoned the nerve to ask her where she could find help.

That lead her to Beat the Street, a program that helps people who are illiterate for all the reasons that befall sad children: unrecognized learning disabilities, emotional stress, too many schools, scorn and belittling, terror, bad teachers. She was linked with a volunteer tutor, and they came to admire each other deeply.

"Now I can read, I can read books, anything. I can write. In English *and* French."

Carole Boudrias has written a book, *The Struggle for Survival*, which tells of her tortured childhood lacerated with incest and violence, and her triumphant recovery from illiteracy. Last summer [1989] she was the poet laureate of the annual golf tournament hosted by Peter Gzowski, the beloved and respected heart of CBC Radio's *Morningside*. He has befriended the cause of literacy in Canada and over the past four years has raised a quarter of a million dollars for Frontier College, one of the first organizations in the country to tackle the problem of illiteracy.

"Learning to read," Carole Boudrias says quietly, "was like a second birth, this time with my eyes open. Before I could read, I was a blind person."

Canada has nearly five million adult citizens who are described as functionally illiterate, which means that they can recognize a few words, such as washroom signs and exits, but they can't read dense print at all. They can't decipher directions, for instance, or application forms, or warnings on labels. The world of newspapers, posters, advertising, books, menus, banking, recipes, and instructions-for-assembly that literate people take for granted is barred to them; they live a life of bluff, anxiety, embarrassment, and isolation.

A good many Canadians are as profoundly illiterate as Carole Boudrias was. People who meet illiterate adults are struck by the similarity of their textural experience. All of them liken the inability to read and write with being disabled or chained in a prison. Edwin Newman, a U.S. broadcaster who writes about language, calls illiteracy "death in life."

The sense of being caged and blinded is not morbid fantasy. People who can't read may be able to walk freely but they can't go far. Subway stops rarely have pictures to guide them and the destinations bannered across the front of buses and streetcars are meaningless. If they ask for directions, well-intentioned people tell them, "Go along Main Street to Elm and turn left." Consequently, they must travel by taxi or stay home, though they usually are the poorest of the poor.

Almost every job, even simple manual labour such as street-cleaning, requires an ability to read. Personnel managers don't take kindly to people who can't fill out an application, or when asked, can't spell their own addresses.

The divide between the literate and illiterate has never been wider. In this half of the century North America has become a world of forms and documents and instructions, written warnings, posted rules, leaflets, and vital information circulated in brochures. Two generations ago, illiteracy was prevalent but not such a great disadvantage. Someone functionally illiterate could fake it through an entire lifetime and still hold a good job. Employment skills were acquired by watching someone else;

apprenticeship was the accepted teacher, not two years in a community college.

Today inability to read is a ticket to social segregation and economic oblivion. A poignant example is the skilled house-painter who turned up one day in the crowded quarters of the East End Literacy Program in Toronto. He said he wanted to read. The counsellor asked him, as all applicants are asked, what he wanted to read. "Directions on paint cans," he answered promptly. "I'm losing jobs. I can't read how to mix the colours."

Many who are illiterate can't read numbers. When they are paid, they don't know if they are being cheated. Because she couldn't fill out bank deposit slips, Carole Boudrias used to cash her welfare cheque in a storefront outlet which clips poor people sharply for no-frills service. To pay for goods, she would hold out a handful of money and let the cashier take what was needed—and perhaps more, she never knew. Once she would have been shortchanged $50 she could ill afford if a stranger who witnessed the transaction hadn't protested.

The common emotional characteristic of people who can't read is depression and self-dislike. All feel at fault for their situation: with few exceptions, they went through school with bright little girls exactly their age who leaped to their feet to recite and smart little boys who did multiplication in their heads. Everyone else in the world, it seemed, could learn with ease; for them, even C-A-T looked a meaningless scribble. Teachers called them stupid; worse, so did other children.

"Stupid" may just be the cruellest word in the language. It consumes confidence, on which the ability to learn relies. Seven-year-olds having trouble with reading will frolic at recess with an edge of glee; 11-year-olds who can't read have bitter faces and scarred souls.

Loss of hope for oneself is a descent into desolation without end. It causes men to rage in fury and women to wound themselves. People who can't read come readily to view themselves as worthless junk, and many feel they must grab what they can out of life and run. Canada's prisons are full of young men who can't read. The Elizabeth Fry Society estimates that close to 90 per cent of the women in Kingston's infamous prison for women are illiterate.

Because Canada has five million people who can't read, the political shape of the country and priorities of governments are not influenced greatly by the needs of the poor. Since illiterates are effectively disenfranchised, the political agenda is written by the more powerful. Candidates rarely find it advantageous to uphold the causes that matter most to Canada's illiterates—an end to homelessness and the need for food banks, welfare payments that meet the poverty line, and better educational and job-training opportunities. Few votes would follow any politician with such a crusade. The electorate that can't read won't be there to ruffle the complacent on election day.

Their silence costs this country severely. Education is free in Canada because it was recognized that democracy isn't healthy unless all citizens understand current events and issues. Five million Canadians can't do that. Voters, most of them literate, choose candidates who help their interests; those who don't vote, many of them illiterate, by default get a government that does not need to know they exist.

The result is a kind of apartheid. The government has lopsided representation, which results in decisions which further alienate and discourage the unrepresented. The gap between the haves and have-nots in Canada is already greater than at any time in this century, and widening. Urban apartment houses are the work places of crack dealers, the streets are increasingly unsafe, and households have installed electronic security systems. The poor, if asked, would have better answers than guard dogs. The best, most lasting responses to crime and addiction and violence are literacy programs, coupled with job training and full employment.

Schools are in disgrace, with a failure rate of fully one-third of all high school students. A soup company with such a record would be out of business in a day. The educational system has managed to exacerbate the class differences which are developing in this country. Canada's millions of illiterates went through school the required number of years, give or take time-out for truancy, illness, running away from abuse, and confinement in detention homes. These human discards, identified promptly in the first years of elementary schools, will ever after drift around disconsolately. They are surplus people, spare parts for which society has no use. Unless there is a war.

Carole Boudrias is working on a project, Moms in Motion, to help young mothers to get off welfare rolls. She says to them, "What do you want?" They reply, "To go back to school."

Another chance. Five million Canadians need another chance. Maybe they can become literate, maybe they can become healed and whole. What a lovely goal for the 1990s.

Activities

1. With a partner, identify five ways in which the essay describes how illiterate people in our society are disadvantaged. Select one of these ways and write a report in which you describe the nature of the disadvantage and the way it might affect a person's ability to earn a living and raise a family.

2. In a journal entry, describe something you enjoy doing that an illiterate person would enjoy doing just as easily. In a second paragraph, describe something you like to do that an illiterate person would be unable to do. In a third paragraph, explain how your daily life would be changed if you could not read or write.

3. With a partner, develop a short dialogue in which an illiterate person has to ask a literate person for assistance. Your dialogue should indicate the setting in which the illiterate person is having difficulty. Present your dialogue to the class. Invite your audience to respond to your dialogue.

4. Write a story or a poem about a teenager or an adult who cannot read and write. Include details in your writing that illustrate the plight of the illiterate in our society.

5. Invite someone who works with illiterate adults to visit your class. Prepare questions in advance that you would like answered. Write up an account of the discussion for the school newspaper that will draw attention to the extent and nature of the problem of illiteracy in your community.

6. Interview a primary teacher to learn more about how children learn to read and why some children struggle with this learning process. Prepare a report on what you learn.

7. Arrange for your class to visit a class of Grade 1 or 2 students to participate in shared reading activities.

End of Unit Activities

1. With a partner, make a list of the official holidays in Canada and the traditional way each is celebrated. Using the criterion that public holidays should help Canadians understand, appreciate, and celebrate their culture and identity, decide which holidays you think should be kept and which should be discarded. Create one holiday for Canadians for each month of the year. In each case, assign a date (either a specific calendar date or a date such as "the first Monday of the month"). Present your calendar of holidays to the class and offer reasons why you feel it should be adopted.

2. Design a travel poster or brochure that you think would attract tourists to Canada. Display it for others to view.

3. In a group of three, research prominent Canadians who have made contributions to the country and to the world in one of the following areas: politics, literature, art, culture, business, research, or scholarship. You might use *The Canadian Encyclopedia* as a reference source. Write an essay about the individual to include in a collection entitled *Great Canadians You Should Know About.*

4. Interview someone who has come to Canada in the past five years from another country. Write a report about the differences he or she sees between the country of his or her birth and Canada. If you were born in another country, write a comparison between the country of your birth and Canada.

5. Arrange for your class to visit a museum, art gallery, or pioneer village that has exhibits on life in Canada. Write a report for publication in the school newspaper about the exhibits you viewed and your response to them.

6. Write a story about the exploits of a fictional Canadian super hero or heroine. You might present your story in the form of a comic book.

7. Debate the following: Be it resolved that the Canadian mosaic theory of society is superior to the American melting pot theory.

8. Write an essay on one of the following topics:
  · what I like about Canada
  · my pet peeve about Canada
  · my favourite Canadian television show or musical group
  · my dream vacation in Canada

The Games of Our Lives

If you can react the same way to winning and losing, that's a big accomplishment. That quality is important because it stays with you the rest of your life, and there's going to be a life after tennis that's a lot longer than your tennis life.

CHRIS EVERT LLOYD,
TENNIS PLAYER

Hockey captures the essence of the Canadian experience in the New World. In a land so inescapably and inhospitably cold, hockey is the dance of life, an affirmation that despite the deathly chill of winter we are alive.

BRUCE KIDD,
RUNNER

The easiest thing in sport(s) is to win when you're good. The next easiest thing is to lose when you're not any good. The hardest thing is to lose when you're good. That's the test of character.

ROY EISENHART,
BASEBALL EXECUTIVE

For me, track and field has been about finding things out about myself, and that will go on as long as I live.

DEBBIE BRILL,
HIGH JUMPER

The Road to a Broader Horizon

Laura Robinson

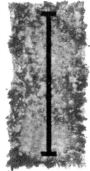

I remember so clearly the day I rode to my first 10-mile [16-km] cycling time trial. I had barely left my house when two other cyclists pulled up to a stoplight beside me. We were headed to the same race. One was a draft dodger from the United States, whose long hair, beard and disdain for anything conservative and American gave away his roots immediately. The other was an Italian from Argentina, whose family had fled the political repression of that country.

Even though I had just turned 14, I felt as if I was riding into a world I had never dreamed of, but could not wait to explore. A kid from the sterile suburbs of Mississauga, Ont., had been given a hint of a foreign, unpredictable and even dangerous world that lay beyond the confines of Southern Ontario.

Duanne and Angelo "adopted" my brother and me. During rides, they waited for us at crossroads when the pace of the rides became too fast for the two youngest members of the cycling club. They told us stories about the places they had grown up in as we rode along the back roads of the province. In winter, they picked us up before dawn and we would head north to the cross-country ski trails and ski until the sun set.

The formative teen-age years were filled with words of encouragement and acts of camaraderie from Duanne and Angelo. Within a couple of years, it was my brother and I waiting for them on the cycle tours and racing away on ski trails, intent on finding out who was faster—brother or sister.

I started taking sport very seriously, and traded in the informal club competitions for the provincial competitive circuit in cycling and skiing. My earlier partners in both sports became fans, yelling at me to not give up, to finish the race, no matter how much it hurt. They were there for the victories and the defeats.

I wanted to do really well. I wanted to be a world champion. I wanted to race all over the world and see whether I could keep up to the really fast women.

I did not realize my dream of being world champion, but I did meet athletes from throughout the world. I was still in Grade 10 when I rode my first race on Mount Royal in Montreal. Quebec loves cyclists. European influences are greater in Quebec and there is not the infatuation with the North American pro sport culture that pumps up the rest of the country.

I found myself in a pack of French-speaking women and, for the first time, realized that dropping French in school was related to how well I would race in Quebec. Eventually, I moved there for the summer so I could race and learn French at the same time.

I crossed borders to the south as well. The American women all seemed so self-assured and confident. While I could barely make it out of the washroom because of pre-race nerves, the American women were joking about as if totally oblivious to the fact that the race was going to start.

I thought all the European women were goddesses; after all, cycling's roots were in the tiny villages and mountain passes of their continent.

Meanwhile, in cycling's off-season, I met the legendary Finns, who huddled together as they concocted the perfect wax combination for their racing skis. Karl, one of the friendly veterans among them, helped me figure out exactly what colours and amounts were to be ironed and rubbed with the utmost care onto my ski base.

Angelo, Duanne, Karl and many others taught me lessons beyond how to lean into a corner or iron on wax. Angelo spoke about the disappearances of his friends and co-workers in Argentina. Duanne angrily denounced the United States and its inability to do anything but carry a big stick. Karl told me about the Finnish Canadians who used to travel from Sault Ste. Marie to Sudbury, camping and skiing for the entire trip, so they could attend the Finnish Workers Games in Northern Ontario.

I wish all kids had people like Angelo, Duanne and Karl in their lives. They were good friends and counsellors. They never seemed to need to drive quickly or drink to prove they were real men. It never crossed my mind to drink, either. I could not imagine doing something to my body that would make it go slower when all I wanted to do was go fast.

Nor did I think of myself as less female because I was healthy and strong. I just felt more me.

Activities

1. With a partner, identify the ways the sport of cycling has enriched the author's life. List your own ideas about ways that participation in sports activities can be satisfying and fulfilling. Be prepared to share your lists with the class.

2. In a journal entry, describe the best and worst experience you have had playing sports.

3. In a group of three, discuss your reasons for believing sports are or are not an important part of the growing up experience. Summarize your thoughts in an oral report to the class.

4. Prepare a bulletin board display on your favourite sport. Include a written report on the reasons why the sport appeals to you.

5. Write a description of
   a) a memorable sports event you attended or participated in

   OR

   b) a person you met through sports whom you will not forget.

   Describe details about the person or event that explain the memorable effect. Share your description with a partner.

The Common Passion

Ken Dryden and Roy MacGregor

n the coldest day of the year—more than forty degrees below by any measure—and in the teeth of what will be described in the morning paper as the worst blizzard to sweep down from Alaska in 100 years, the Yellowhead Highway is all but devoid of life. Cars and trucks travelling between Saskatoon and the Battlefords have been abandoned where they spun blind. Outside Radisson, within sight of the large red and white and black sign that in determined letters reads "Town With a Future!" there is only a rented car crawling uncertainly on black ice and, high above the slick road, a solitary black raven.

Ugly and naked on the cold wind, the bird drifts oblivious to the sheets of snow that flick off the near fields. But this is the raven, renowned for its ability to survive impossible conditions, an opportunist of enormous cunning. This is *Tuluguk*, the wise bird who, the Inuit say, created light by flinging mica chips against the sky, the one who dared to try what no one else had even imagined—and who succeeded against all odds.

Opposite the big sign sits the Red Bull Café, a combination gas station, video rental, and restaurant that serves as the Radisson "coffee row," a highway coffee and doughnut stand that is charged, along with the elevator and arena, with the care and nurturing of the town's soul. "Coffee row," Saskatchewan poet Stephen Scriver has written, "this is where it's at...if you want to find out about your past, present, or future, here it'll be...."

And here, on a "dangerously cold" winter's day between harvest and seeding, local men—no women—have come to the Red Bull Café to talk, as always, about hockey. Usually, the talk is about last night's NHL schedule of games, especially about the Gretzky-less Edmonton Oilers if they happened to play,

sometimes about the local junior team, Saskatoon's Blades of
the Western Hockey League, just sixty kilometres down the
highway. But more often now, they talk about their own hockey
future. Radisson's old rink has been condemned as structurally
unsafe. And in their voices, there is a mixture of fear for their
community if they cannot raise the money necessary to build
a new one, and hope that as they and their ancestors have done
so often before, they will somehow find a way.

Radisson has "434 people on an early Sunday morning,"
according to the local school principal, Walter Kyliuk, who stirs
his coffee while his neighbours burst, stomping and wheezing,
through a glass door that has been painted solid with frost.
Gathering here is the team that runs a typical Saskatchewan
town with a Pool elevator, a Massey-Ferguson dealership, a post
office, a fire hall, Co-op, Red & White, hotel, one boarded-up
store, a ball diamond with local advertisers—"Bronsch Auctions";
"John Gerich MLA, Working for You for a Better Tomorrow"—
providing the home-run fence, and a pool hall that prefers to
say "Billiards" over its entrance.

If one thing sets Radisson off from the hundreds of other
small towns in the province, it is the nearly billboard-size sign
at the turn by the farm equipment dealership, a painting of a
Buffalo Sabres hockey player with the proud words "Welcome
to Radisson, Home of Bill Hajt"—the home town honouring
the local boy who went off down the Yellowhead Highway to
play for the Saskatoon Blades, and from there to the National
Hockey League. If there is one thing that ties Radisson to those
other freckles across the face of Saskatchewan, it is that its
arena—where Bill Hajt first learned to play his game—has been
declared uninsurable.

"If you lose the rink," says Scotty Mundt, the retired power
company employee who now as a volunteer takes care of the
town arena, "people'll lose interest in the town and start looking
other places. It's just as important as the elevator."

"It's the backbone of the community," says Don Harris, who
runs the elevator. "That's what draws people to the town."

Around the tables, the coffee spoons stir and the men nod.
"We know of other towns that have lost their rinks," says
Kyliuk. "They die overnight. It's the grand central gathering

place for the young and the old. The young come to skate and the older citizens come in to watch. The arena is the gathering place for the winter months."

"It's a baby-sitting place, too," adds Alfons Hajt, who, as Bill's father, has a particular place of honour at the Red Bull Café, a status that remains even though his son retired from professional hockey in 1987 after fourteen seasons with the Sabres. "Families like to leave the kids there and they'll do something else. And the children? They know they're looked after. They have a place to go."

"If I'd known that when they asked me to take on the rink," says Mundt with a wink, "I wouldn't be looking after it now." His friends laugh.

Dave Roberts listens and nods knowingly beneath his wide cowboy hat as these men from Radisson talk about the rink's value to their community. Roberts comes from Fielding, the next village up the Yellowhead Highway. "The first thing to go was our hockey rink," he says finally. "Then our curling rink went. Then our grocery stores started to go and gradually the school went and then our post office. All we have left now is a community hall which gets used once or twice a year for a stag party or a meeting....Three families live in Fielding now and the rest is all deserted empty buildings."

Coffee row goes silent but for the ring of spoons being lazily turned. Roberts offers a vision more horrible to contemplate than the blizzard that bullies at the café door, daring them to come back out into a storm where even the raven must go with the prevailing winds.

Sixty kilometres east of Radisson, cars and half-tons are crawling along the Yellowhead where Highway 16 connects with 12. They move so slowly it is possible to hear the knock-knock that comes from tires that have been squared frozen on one edge as they sat through a day in which the radio warns that "exposed flesh will freeze in less than one minute." Thirteen deaths across the Prairies have already been attributed to the storm's cold and snow. A young farmer's truck has quit within sight of a farmhouse and yet he has frozen to death before he could walk the short distance. The radio stations have turned over their regular programming to endless lists of cancellations. *No bingo this*

*evening at the Elks club...no Brownies at All Saints...Parent-
teachers meeting put off 'til next Monday... curling cancelled until
the weekend.* And the radio stations have filled in the spaces with
incoming calls from listeners who are trapped in farmhouses
and homes from Meadow Lake to Maymont, prairie people who
talk about the food and fuel they have on hand as proof that the
elements will never beat them, no matter what. *No 4-H
tonight...no dart tournament...cribbage cancelled...choir practice
off...*

But out here on the Yellowhead Highway on the northern
outskirts of Saskatoon, the road is plugged with idling, blinking
cars spewing exhaust smoke as thick as toothpaste. In this unlikely place on this forbidding night, the vehicles' occupants are
almost in reach of their evening's destination, Saskatchewan Place.
They park in the paved field that surrounds the arena, then
hurry through wind and blowing snow and air so cold nostrils
lock solid on a single breath. They are going to a hockey game.

Inside, they will cheer when the scoreboard flashes
"COMPLIMENTARY BOOSTS AFTER THE GAME—
BRIDGE CITY TOWING" and they will cheer again—
proudly—during the third period when the game's attendance is
announced: 5,594. They have come to the brand-new SaskPlace
arena on a night when "extreme caution is advised," come to
watch a junior hockey game featuring the third-place Saskatoon
Blades and the seventh-place Regina Pats. They have come to
cheer the progress of their home-town team as they go through
a season-long training camp toward May's Memorial Cup, the
Canadian championship for Junior A hockey. Saskatoon has
never before been host city, the Blades, awarded an automatic
berth as host team of the championships, never before a finalist.

And they have come to cheer for prairie kids with distinctly
Canadian names, like Katelnikoff and Kocur, Snesar, Kuntz,
Holoien, Lelacheur, Bauer, Yellowaga, Smart, and Sutton. And
to wait for a nineteen-year-old named Kevin Kaminski—a
young man with blue eyes and black, curling hair now skating
about the warm-up with his sweater tucked big-league style into
the left side of his pants—once again to strut his stuff.

They have come to a $30-million state-of-the-art hockey rink
where the first sod was turned by a ninety-three-year-old World

War One veteran named Johnny Walker, who as a young boy skated miles along the Qu'Appelle River with a rifle in his hand rather than a hockey stick, in search of mink not pucks. And they have come to drink Labatt's Blue beer in public in a city founded more than a century ago by the Temperance Colonization Society with the stated goal of creating a community where alcoholic beverages would never, ever be served. But they have not come to remind themselves of whom they are or how far they have come or how much they have changed along the way. They have come for the same reason people in Saskatchewan have always come to arenas: to be together.

Saskatoon's Wild Bill Hunter, who would turn this building into a home for a National Hockey League team if only the gods would listen to reason, says that on any winter Friday, Saturday, or Sunday night in the province of Saskatchewan—population slightly in excess of one million—more than 300,000 of these citizens are watching a live hockey game in some community, be it Saskatoon or Kevin Kaminski's home town of Churchbridge. And even if Hunter occasionally deals more in exuberant truths than in more earthbound literal facts, the point is the same. Here, people love this game, and once more this damnable evening they prove it.

It is a mythic Canadian night. The land, the winter are everywhere. People are out where they shouldn't be, doing what to others seems to make no sense. But for the original prairie settlers, for Bill Hunter and Kevin Kaminski, for the people of tiny Radisson, for Canadians, what did sense ever have to do with anything?

Canada is such an improbable country. Just how improbable can be seen from an airplane drifting into Saskatoon's airport, just a few river-hockey games away from SaskPlace. The immensity of the land overwhelms. Only a few scruffs of trees and buildings distract the eye from its utter space. The land separates and disconnects, place from place, person from person. What links it all together seems so hopelessly overmatched. The broad winding rivers that brought in fur traders, the ruler-straight railway lines that brought settlers in and their grain out, the highways, the power lines, the TV antennae and TV dishes—such fragile threads to bind this far-flung land and its people. All serve to connect in some way, but these cannot create the bond. What ties us together must be a feeling that travels the waters and pavement and airwaves and steel: things we have in common, things we care about, things that help us make sense out of what we are.

It is a hard-won feeling. So much about Canada sets us apart—distance, topography, climate, language, European rivalries and cultures. The country can seem so contrary to destiny and good sense that at times we ask ourselves, "Why bother?" Canada has never worked seriously at developing the traditional instruments of community: the icons of nationhood—flag, constitution, monument—the myths, legendary figures, events and commemorative dates. Without such evidences of nation worship, without focal points for community expression, it can seem we lack a sense of nation. It can seem that what sets us apart is stronger than what holds us together. It can make our bonds seem frail. It can make us weak when we are not.

It matters little what the icon is, what the myth is about. For American nationhood, a bronze statue, the Statue of Liberty, is important, a story about a future President and a cherry tree gets passed on from generation to generation. An icon is nothing more than a symbol. It embodies and evokes what a nation feels about itself and offers its people the too-rare opportunity to express what they really feel. Canadians may seem undemonstrative and reserved, but not at a hockey game. We may seem isolated and distinct one from another, we may seem non-patriotic, but not at a hockey game. Hockey helps us express what we feel about Canada, and ourselves. It is a giant point of contact, in a place, in a time, where we need every one we have—East and West, French and English, young and old, past and present. The winter, the land, the sound of children's voices, a frozen river, a game—all are part of our collective imaginations. Hockey makes Canada feel more Canadian.

And it is here in Saskatchewan, this most Canadian of provinces, that we look for a game in its place.

Activities

1. With a partner, check the meaning of the words *icon*, *myth*, and *symbol* in a dictionary. Discuss whether you would agree with the authors that hockey is an icon of Canadian culture and if there are other icons that might represent Canada as well. Compare your ideas with those of another partnership.

2. In a group of three, consider a place in your community where a conversation similar to the one that took place at the Red Bull Café in Radisson, Saskatchewan, might occur. Write your own version of the conversation that might take place. Include references to local sports teams and details about them. Share the conversation you develop with other groups.

3. Check a television guide and the sports pages of a local paper to learn which sports have the major media attention and coverage for a week. In a group of three, discuss ideas about the criteria media sports departments use for establishing which events are profiled and how much space or time is provided.

4. In a journal entry, describe an experience you have had related to hockey. You might write about a game you saw, played, or heard about.

Lightning in Your Heart

Angella Issajenko
as told to Martin O'Malley and Karen O'Reilly

n Jamaica, the teachers at the high school
encouraged us to get involved in extracurricular
activities, mainly sports, and a lot of the kids
joined netball teams. It is a British game,
patterned after basketball but played with a
soccer ball. It is tremendously popular in the
Caribbean, where both men and women play it.

After classes, I started going out to the
track and field events. I gravitated to running.
Running really is a pretty ungainly thing to do
if you're trying to impress the boys. You grunt and sweat a lot,
you fall on your ass, and most girls consider this too big a risk.
Eventually I was the only senior girl in the school to run.

We ran barefoot on grass in lanes marked with lime.
Sometimes two people would hold a thread across the finish
line. One time when I was running they didn't let go of the
thread in time and it slashed my neck. It took me a while to get
over that; I guess it's like a rider who's thrown off a mount, or a
diver who hits the board. I can laugh about it now, that fear of
the finish line. Years later, in Canada, my trainer designed a
series of exercises for me so I would keep my back from arching
at the finish line. He wanted my upper chest to break the tape.

Most of the time, I ran 150-metre sprints. There were no
starting blocks, just a standing start. Sometimes they'd fire a gun
to start the race, but what I remember most is the grass. The
intramural races were held on weekends, and I liked to arrive
early on Saturday mornings so I could sit on the grass and watch
the phys ed teachers prepare the field, which always involved
trimming the grass. The adults were like different people those

weekends, more relaxed, calling jokes to one another. There never was a more peaceful time in my life than those mornings when the grass was still wet with dew. The smell of freshly cut grass has an evocative hold on me. It's a childhood fragrance, and just a whiff of it on a summer morning in Toronto carries me back to those Saturdays at the track on the island.

We were still running for powder puffs, occasionally a ribbon or a medal. I once competed in an all-girls final in our district, but I didn't win. I don't remember being disappointed, though I began to like winning.

I have often thought about that feeling, moments before the race, when the starter says, "On your mark...." I find it nearly erotic. It's the adrenaline, sure, but there's more. It's an unbearable mix of fear and excitement, of lightning in your heart, and you can feel it flash to the nerve ends. It's a feeling of—ignition. It is what a champion feels.

In high school, I couldn't even eat before a race. It was as though I was already too intensely alive. It's a distillation, a synthesis, of fierce energy, pure life. No one can touch it, add to it, take away from it. It's a natural high and your body gives it to you.

I dedicated more time to my running, but not for any world-class dreams or lofty aspirations. It just made me feel good, and at school I was beginning to feel that my life was taking shape. I had made it into high school and I was adjusting to the idea of school as home. That's when I considered engineering as a career. I knew that with a profession, the island is a fine place to live, even for a woman. I enrolled in "shops," courses in woodworking and metalworking.

I also had won some cachet among my classmates because my mother was in Canada. I still considered my grandmother in England my real mother, but it was nice to know that Olive Bird [Issajenko's mother] could cause a stir. In the island, one automatically assumes that life will be better if you leave. They call it "going abroad." Everyone wants to go abroad.

I've seen this on other Caribbean islands, too, as I did when we trained in Guadeloupe. There, they all wanted to go to New York. And it's not unique to the Caribbean; when I competed in Communist countries, I found everyone wanted to go to America, where the money grows on trees. That's how most

Jamaicans see Canada and the United States. I didn't, not then. I felt I had a future in Jamaica. I thought I was on my way.

When I was thirteen, one of the phys ed teachers took an interest in me. I can't remember her name, but she was a black woman, about six feet [180 cm] tall, and she had pale, yellowy skin. We weren't buddies—students kept a respectful distance from teachers—but she used to watch me run those times I competed in the weekend races. She urged me to run in intramural and district meets against other schools. At the end of my second year, I returned home for the summer to live with Hilda [a great-aunt of Issajenko] and her family and I had been home only about a week when this teacher called me back to Clarendon. She wanted me to run in an all-Jamaica high school championship meet in Kingston.

I had never been to Kingston, the capital of Jamaica. In those days, the fairy tale picture that came into my head for any strange, faraway place I had never been to was the Land of Oz— Dorothy and the yellow brick road.

I boarded one of those old, dusty buses that lumber through the countryside and traveled back to Clarendon to visit my phys ed teacher in the big house she shared with some other teachers. I stayed with them overnight, so we could set out for Kingston early in the morning. I was the only athlete she had chosen from the school. Maybe the others weren't good enough or maybe they weren't interested, but it made me feel special to be the only one she picked to go to Kingston.

We left at daybreak in a car the teacher had borrowed from a friend. Heading down the road, just the two of us, I felt very grown up. And I felt like I was going to the end of the earth. I had never been more than twenty miles [32 km] from my home.

As we neared Kingston, driving by the curve of the harbor, I saw my first sailing boats. There were fair-weather clouds, but the morning already was hot and steamy. The boats were far off in the distance, bobbing on the water, the sun catching their sails. They looked like swans.

And Kingston! I'd never imagined an Oz like this. The streets were crowded with people, and cars and buses and trucks and wagons. Bicycles clattered by. Policemen blew their whistles. People haggled at the open markets, people of all shapes, sizes, and colors. Some wore suits and ties, some wore turbans, bright saffron robes, or saris. And there were young guys in bushy Afros, thick combs stuck out of the back pockets of their jeans. From the sidewalks and bars I could hear steel-band music, rock, reggae. Even in the car, my feet wanted to dance.

My favorite weather always has been a tropical storm. Storms break the monotony in the countryside. They can be dangerous, for sure, but they're an honest enemy. They howl and lash at you, they push against the windows and bend the trees nearly to the ground, but when they've blown out to sea the air is always fresh and tangy. It feels as though something's been resolved, like something *happened*. Kingston was like a tropical storm that you made yourself, with crowds and music. It felt as if you could have one any time you wanted. That's what it was like in Kingston—something was happening.

I didn't know the world could get that hot. The heat seemed to rise from the streets, as if the city itself was baking. Sweat dripped from my face. I was hungry, but I couldn't think of eating. I was too excited. The teacher had a friend in Kingston and we drove there and lounged around the house before going to the stadium. All the time, I was aware that I was the reason we were there, waiting for my race at the stadium. My race was scheduled for late in the afternoon.

The stadium was enormous, a great bowl of people. It was the national stadium, regularly used for soccer. The high-jumpers and long-jumpers and discus-throwers were doing their grunty things in the field, which was encircled by the running track. The stands were filled to the sky with people, waves of people dressed in all the colors of the spectrum. And there was this constant, raucous murmur, as if you were standing at the edge of the sea. Sometimes I wonder how big that stadium would look to me today.

Funny, but standing there, trying to take everything in, my eyes began to focus on individuals in the mass of people in the stands. There were a lot of women in white T-shirts and blue denim jeans and skirts—I guess it was the style of the day—but what caught my eye were the women wearing lime green. Some of the athletes were even wearing lime green shorts. They just seemed to look more comfortable in lime green. Probably it was because of the heat, but that's when I made the connection between something fashionable and something "cool." I made a mental note to write Grandmother Vasthie in England and ask for a lime green blouse.

My attention wandered to the athletes, many of whom wore shorts made of a shiny, plastic-looking material. They had matching tank tops that they called singlets. The material made them look unnaturally sleek, like something out of a magazine. Some of the girls had fancy elastics with colored plastic balls attached to hold back their hair. Then I noticed the running shoes. They looked strangely exotic, with bright colors and stripes and high sides that covered the ankles. On the track, the athletes wore shoes with spikes.

I walked over to the edge of the track, which didn't look like any track I'd ever seen before. It was incredibly long; I could barely see the far curve. It must have been a standard 400-metre track, but I had never run on anything longer than 150 metres. At school, after crossing the finish line, we just ran off the track and came to a stop in a field of tall grass.

I wasn't going to be running on grass that afternoon. I wasn't sure what I would be running on, but it sure wasn't grass. I had never seen a track like the one at the stadium in Kingston. It was even, brick-colored, hard and mean-looking in the sun. I knelt down and pushed my fingers on the track, and it pushed back. Rubberized! I know now that it must have been either Chevron or Tartan, trade names for a synthetic resin surface that was originally invented for horse racing in the United States.

I couldn't have been the only one in Kingston astounded by the track that day. The first time a Tartan track had been used in the Olympic Games was in 1968 in Mexico. Before that, tracks were made of cinder or clay, or any available dirt. I can't remember how many lanes were marked off that afternoon in Kingston, or even how fast I thought I could run on that springy, rust-colored track; all I kept thinking was that I would stub my toe on it badly. I was going to run in my bare feet, the way I'd run on the grass at home and on the field those Saturday mornings in Clarendon.

For the first time that day, I heard the hollow, disembodied voice of a public-address announcer, and it sounded like every other competitor was named Scott. As it turned out, it was only one person, another woman runner. This girl Scott seemed to be entered in every event. Everyone was cheering for her. And she was winning everything—100-metres, 200-metres, long jump. She was a big, muscular girl, yet she moved with tremendous grace and power. I was spellbound. When she passed once I was so close to the track that I could hear her breathing—sharp, guttural grunts. I could see the determination in her face, the concentration. She exuded a kind of passionate pain and rapture I had never seen before. But then, I had never seen a woman like her before.

I was then about the same height as I am now, five feet, six inches [165 cm]. I wore my hair in two pigtails, held with elastic bands. No makeup—I was still a grubesse. I wore my school phys ed outfit, one of those heavily starched skorts.

I didn't warm up for my race. I never had before, so why bother now? I just slipped my shoes off and I was ready to go. Then I saw the starting blocks.

I have my own set of blocks today, but back then, my God, they looked like some carpenter's tool. They're a shaft of aluminum, about four feet [1.4 m] long, with two angled blocks attached that you can adjust to fit the length of your legs, for your crouch at the start. They have long spikes underneath that fasten to the track, so you can push off, like you're pushing off from a curb.

You need the blocks for a start, yet there's a lot of technique, too, and some runners are just better at it than others. I was never a terrific starter. For most of my career my strength was finishing, accelerating. Ben Johnson, BJ, could explode from the blocks.

There was a movie in the early 1980s called *Personal Best*, about women athletes preparing for the Olympics, and Mariel Hemingway plays a rookie who has never used starting blocks. In the hurdles, when she pushes off for the first time, she falls flat on her face. That's probably what would have happened to me if I'd used the blocks that afternoon.

I was entered in the 150-metre race. All I can remember is the sound of the starting pistol. After that, it was like every other race I've ever run before or since—a complete silence overtakes me. I hear nothing of the spectators, I feel nothing but air beneath my feet, I see nothing but the finish line.

And even that was different on this day in Kingston. It was an official tape, stretched between two poles with no one holding it. The girl in front of me, whose name was Jacqueline Pusey, broke it on her chest.

I came second. I don't remember what the prize was, but I do remember thinking that I was used to winning, and I had lost.

Activities

1. With a partner, decide which three statements suggest the young Angella Issajenko had "the right stuff" to become a world class runner. Discuss the quality that each statement revealed.

2. Select a section of the essay that particularly appeals to you. Explain to a partner why you think that section is so effective.

3. Write an editorial for the school newspaper on some issue that concerns or interests you about the intramural or extra-curricular athletic programs at your school.

4. In your journal,
   a) write your thoughts about the life and experience of a world class athlete you admire

   OR

   b) write an entry that begins "If I could be a professional athlete, I'd be...."

5. A "Snoopy" poster has a caption that reads, "If it doesn't matter whether you win or lose, why do they keep score?" A famous football coach once said, "Winning isn't everything. It's the only thing." Write your response to either one (or both) of these statements. In a group of three, share your writings. Prepare a chart listing points made in favour of or against each statement.

Student Writing

The Skier

Nancy Dorey

nder the fetal warmth of a heavy quilt, muscles stretch and groan, sore from yesterday's turns and and spills. The room is dark; outside it's snowing. Sweaty ski clothes are waiting to be put on again. An early morning breakfast is eaten in haste. Stiff boots must once again encase sore feet before you can venture out into the astounding silence of falling snow. You wade through it, shin deep, boots crunching, skis on shoulder; the whole world is white.

The lift is silent and snow covered. You are early. And so, with cold feet and impatience, you share the falling snow with a few others, all waiting while stomping their feet to keep warm.

The lift operator arrives and is soon sweeping snow off the lift with an overworked broom. White fluff scatters in clouds to reveal dark, greasy metal. A cough, a hum, gears clank, and the chairs lurch into motion, beginning their daily, repetitive journey. The operator nods and you slide into place; the chair comes and you glide upward into the still descending snow.

The silent spruce are black against the sombre sky. Suddenly, there's a hint of blue and the falling snow is thinner now. You watch as a single crystal fairy dances down from the sky; another taps you on the nose.

The sky is blue now, the distant peaks etched silver against it. Three more towers and you are in the sun. The ramp arrives and your skis cut through the ridges as you slide off the chair, down into two feet [60 cm] of sparkling virgin snow. You struggle through the drift, then begin working your skis through the wind-packed snow towards the mountain's lip. Looking down, you see the quick, easy runs below, and above, the more remote slopes still lost in the tattered patch of a cloud that remains in the lee of the mountain. You start creeping upward. The track is long gone; you must guess a line and begin the long journey to the top.

Morning sweat, grunts, and four-letter words abound. The sky is a dazzling blue; the snow sparkles. You go slowly, picking up one ski at a time, stomping down a place for it, then shifting upward one step. Progress is slow, and in places it seems nonexistent.

Struggling still; the lower slopes are distant now; the top still hides. Sweat, sunglare and aching muscles—what a way to start the day—but on you go, thrashing upwards.

The top draws near—edging slowly, so slowly, closer. Sweat has collected around your waist; clothing half on, half off, goggles up one minute and down the next, eyes squinting into the glare and distance. The final few feet take forever: finally you collapse, panting, exhausted, in the snow.

On the ridge the wind is cutting and stray snow sandpapers your face. Beneath your feet the mountain drops away. Amid the silver minarets of the Canadian Rockies you whisper a chant and contemplate your first turn: that first soft sifting of snow, mind and body. On the very edge you hesitate, lost in the mountains, snow and sky. Finally goggles come down; bindings are checked. No words are spoken.

Softly you are away. You turn gently, slowly, then turn again. Turns, more turns, each one like a waltz. You watch the slow arc of arm and pole, feel the flex, turn and twist of muscles and tendons as you come down the mountain. Your skis are free, arcing around and down into the snow again, creating a fine wave that washes up and over you.

One final steep pitch and you land in an explosion of snow. This time the snow is very deep and you are seconds emerging from it. The surface of the snow is fluid. Whiteness surrounds you again—where is up? Where is the mountaintop? Where is down? Where are you going? Will you survive?

Down and down, through the last few remaining turns to the bottom. The last turn, you carve it wide and slow, coming around to look back up the mountain.

Soon others arrive and walk across the flat ground and into the crowd. There in the middle of the mechanical madness of a big-time ski resort you stop, skis on your shoulder, and lose yourself in the wonder of skiing.

Activities

1. With a partner, select three descriptive sentences in this essay and discuss what makes the descriptions so effective. Compare your sentences and ideas with those of two other partnerships.

2. In a journal entry, write about a recreational or sports activity you pursue for enjoyment and/or fitness. Include an assessment of how fit you are and what you might do to become more fit.

3. Write a descriptive essay about the sport you know best. Include details that describe the features of the sport that make it so appealing to you.

4. Create a picture or collage illustrating how you feel about your favourite sport to display on the bulletin board.

Controversy Corner

Team Sports Merely Glorify Violence, Greed

Michele Landsberg

kay, don't take it from me. I'm prejudiced against aggressive team sports. My father was a football player who spent his adult life predicting the weather from the pain in his bashed-up knees. I grew up listening to his roars of approval ("Kill 'em! Smash that S.O.B.!") as he watched TV football. Naturally, I defined my ideal of masculinity in absolute opposition to him.

But quite aside from my personal biases, consider the mounting evidence that organized sports and the sports mentality—from little kids' leagues to college teams to TV spectacle—have become a major cultural pollutant.

The New York Times reported that college athletes are more likely than other students to commit gang rape, and less likely (because they are heroes) to be charged or convicted. *The Village Voice* last week [January 29, 1991] observed that Super Bowl Sunday is "the worst day of the year for domestic violence." And everyone has noticed, and commented on, the disturbing overlap of sports and military lingo.

My question is: why do we put up with it? Why do so many mothers meekly transform themselves into hockey handmaidens, sacrificing sleep, leisure time and family meals so that their sons can grow up in that belligerent culture? Why do we condone our spouses' or children's massive TV indoctrination into glorified aggression and greed?

I called John McMurtry, once a professional football player (for the Calgary Stampeders) and now a philosophy professor at the University of Guelph and one of our most incisive analysts of sport. He reminisced about the thrilling freedom of "shinny" and other spontaneous forms of youthful sport, which he called "the amnesiac subcurrent of our national life.

"But the more there are external pay-offs—fame, glory or money—the more extreme the pathologies that are generated by the imposed structure," he said. "I mean things like violence, hatred, cheating, drugs and authoritarianism."

McMurtry has written about the "striking similarities between football and political fascism: Mass-gathering hysteria, absolute obedience to higher authority, fawning idolization of the powerful…violent aggression against opponents…" He noted that football, like fascism, grounds itself in "the property-seizing principle."

McMurtry rejects the idea that violent games are a necessary outlet for "natural" male aggression. "What organized football did to me," he wrote, "was make me suppress my natural urges and re-express them in an alienating, vicious form. Spontaneous desires for free bodily exuberance and fraternization with competitors were shamed and forced under…and in their place were demanded armored mechanical moves and cool hatred of all opposition."

Fans are not spared this sinister warping, in McMurtry's opinion: "The whole show just further develops and titillates the North American addiction for violent self-assertion."

In a way, our team athletes are offered up to the crowds as human sacrifices. McMurtry remembers winning the most cheers when he physically damaged an opposing player.

Jim Christoff, a Toronto teacher and former pro football player, agrees. "The average life expectancy of an NFL player is 53 years," he wryly points out. He advises parents not to let their kids join hockey teams, and sent me a batch of amazing quotations. Here are a few:

Stephen Crane, author of the powerful Civil War novel *The Red Badge of Courage*, explained in an 1897 letter to a friend, "Of course, I have never been in a battle, but I believe I got my sense of the rage of conflict on the football field."

Red Smith, a famous New York sports writer, decried the repellent "carnival of nationalism" surrounding the Olympics.

He wanted flags, anthems and all team sports eliminated.

George Orwell wrote wistfully about the lost fun of childhood athletics. By contrast, he wrote, in any organized team game "the most savage combative instincts are aroused." Sport is "mimic warfare...an unfailing cause of ill will. Serious sport has nothing to do with fair play. It is bound up with hatred, jealousy, boastfulness, disregard of all rules and sadistic pleasure in witnessing violence..."

"Watching well-advertised strong men knock other people around, make them hurt, is in the end like other tastes. It does not weaken with feeding...It grows," McMurtry wrote in an article 20 years ago. The decades have witnessed the truth of his remarks.

Any thoughtful person watching the current sick inter-twining of jingoism, war frenzy and commercialized sports must be troubled. This is a twisted religion.

"If you can't beat 'em in the alley, you can't beat 'em on the ice," said Conn Smythe. For those of us who do not believe in beating anyone, the question must be: how can we delegitimize this North American ceremony of blood and conquest?

McMurtry says his two athletic sons refuse to participate in any institutionalized sport. That seems like a sensible beginning. Now and then, when you observe youngsters amusing themselves without an audience or a prize, you can see the real spirit of sports: the fun, the exhilaration, the joy and self-forgetfulness of a physical challenge freely undertaken.

Activities

1. With a partner,
   - locate three pieces of information that indicate Michele Landsberg researched her topic,
   - identify any points in the essay you would have liked to learn more about.

2. In a group of three, determine which arguments in the essay you think are the strongest and the weakest. Justify your choices to other groups.

3. Prepare an outline of this essay. For each paragraph in the essay, identify the topic sentence. Using your outline, report to the class whether you feel the essay is well organized.

4. Write out the thesis of this essay in a single sentence beginning, "In this essay the author is trying to prove that..."

5. With a partner, list the negative factors Michele Landsberg attributes to team sports. Make your own list of the positive effects of playing team sports. Using the two lists, decide whether you think team sports should be abolished at your school. Be prepared to report and defend your decision to the class.

6. In a group of three, prepare a short dramatic presentation to illustrate the observation that Super Bowl Sunday is "the worst day of the year for domestic violence." Before you perform for the class, establish the setting, the dialogue, and the outcome for your enactment.

Point/Counterpoint

Should Boys and Girls Play Together on Sports Teams?

(Pro) Helen Lenskyj
(Con) Fran Rider

When 10-year-old Torontonian Justine Blainey lost patience with the short playing season and limited ice time in her all-girls hockey league in 1983, she tried out and qualified for a boys' team. Sport officials cried foul, citing regulations that bar female players from boys' leagues unless there is no girls' league available to them. In 1985, Blainey, charging sexual discrimination, began a two-year legal battle for her right to play.

In December of 1987, a board of inquiry appointed under the Ontario Human Rights Code ruled in Blainey's favor, but similar cases may follow in other provinces. Does equality in sport demand full integration? Or do biological differences mean second-class status for girls who join the boys?

Pro

 he sign on the boys' clubhouse reads, "No girls allowed." Boys play street hockey while girls watch. Male athletes in the locker room act like 10-year-olds when female reporters appear. This is the wide world of sport: masculinity and machismo. Why would any girl or woman want to join it? Why not play on the girls' team instead?

Like most women's issues, it's a question of choices, equal opportunity and, fundamentally, human rights. And it's not simply an either/or debate. Girls should have access to both boys' and girls-only teams. Integrated sport should be an option for the qualified girls and women who want it, and at the same time girls' and women's sports should receive equitable government funding.

Many opponents of integrated sport argue that, if girls are allowed access to boys' teams, girls' teams will have to accept qualified boys. But this is where the affirmative-action clauses of human-rights codes enter the picture by allowing one-way integration.

Simply stated, a goal of human-rights legislation is to correct injustices suffered by disadvantaged groups. Anyone who doubts that girls and women are disadvantaged in sport need only look at the allocation of funds, facilities and equipment in high-school sports, or the media coverage of professional sports, to see that the female stream is not "separate but equal"—it's separate and second-class. In the 1988 Winter Olympics, there were 16 sporting events for women and 28 for men, and male athletes outnumbered women by more than three to one. Accordingly, it is consistent with the intent of human-rights codes to give girls and women access to male-dominated fields, such as sport, but at the same time to protect the athletic programs that have been developed for girls and women only.

When the Canadian Association for the Advancement of Women and Sports (C.A.A.W. & S.) announced its support of Justine Blainey in 1985, opponents of integrated sport attacked these "radicals" for introducing feminist politics into sport. Yet, sport was a feminist issue long before the Blainey case, and the advances that female athletes have made over the past 25 years owe much to the women's movement. As a result of women's lobbying, schools, universities and sports associations now offer more events for girls and women, from junior soccer tournaments to the Olympic marathon. And the jump in female participation rates has been astounding.

Sixty years ago, it was widely believed that girls and women should be protected from the physical and mental strain of traditionally male sports. Strenuous activities would damage the reproductive organs, conventional wisdom held, and competition would promote personality traits—daring, initiative, independence, self-confidence—incompatible with the femininity required of a good wife and mother.

The myths of female frailty have been laid to rest, but traditional notions of femininity still dictate which sports are socially approved for girls and women. Interest in rough-

and-tumble games is seen as just a passing tomboy phase, to be outgrown when girls discover designer jeans, training bras and boys. At this stage, so the argument goes, girls should switch to more feminine activities, where esthetics are as important as athletics: figure skating, not speed skating; synchronized swimming, not triathlons.

But in fact, many young women, like Justine Blainey, shrug off this kind of advice. They simply don't experience any conflict between playing hockey and being a normal teen-age girl. So why are we putting up barriers?

Some women in sport leadership fear that integration will threaten the future of female sport. They point out that the girls' team might lose its best players to the integrated team. But this is the inevitable trade-off when the individual and group interests conflict. The best girl on the team might choose to leave in order to concentrate on her schoolwork or her violin practice. In these cases, she would not be criticized for jeopardizing the future of girls' hockey. As a player, she certainly has a stake in the future of girls' sport, but she does not have an obligation to stay.

There are women in sport leadership who argue that the distinctive features of the female stream would be co-opted if integration occurs. In women's hands, they claim, sport would not develop the bad habits that mar male competition, such as elitism, violence and a winner-at-all costs mentality.

But let's remember that world politics did not change in women's hands. The women who become leaders in politics or sport are unlikely to be the most progressive feminists you know. After all, they are working in a male-dominated field, and many survive by allying themselves with conservative men rather than with trailblazing women.

Your daughter might have a Gloria Steinem coaching her team, or she might have a Margaret Thatcher. The key lies in the value system, not the gender, of the sports leader. And if that sports leader is genuinely concerned about your daughter's right to equal opportunity in sport, he or she will support the option of playing on an integrated team.

Con

Full integration for all ages and in all sports will mean drastically reduced opportunities for female athletes. With uncontrolled emigration of girls to boys' teams, girls' teams will fold, and many girls unwilling or unable to compete with boys will have no chance to play. This is equality?

Sports-minded girls already have enough trouble honing their abilities. Too often, boys' teams monopolize both practice time and funding dollars. But the way to correct such problems is to promote and develop a female sports system leading to Olympic competition and professional events. This effort is now well underway.

Time was when girls either played against boys or hung up their hockey skates. As recently as the mid-'70s, 10-year-old goalie Gail Cummings of Huntsville, Ont., had no girls' team available to her and was rejected by a boys' team because of her sex. The Ontario Women's Hockey Association (O.W.H.A.) helped Cummings take her cause to the Ontario Human Rights Commission. Although she lost, girls have since gained the right to play on boys' teams when no local girls' teams exist. They have also gained teams of their own that equal or even surpass the boys' in coaching and caliber of competition—and are much more sportsmanlike to boot.

Take the teams open to Justine Blainey. The Toronto and surrounding area offers the world's best female hockey opportunities, ranging from provincial championship teams at the novice (girls age 9 and up) level up through the senior A Team Canada, which captured the McCallion World Cup in 1987.

Blainey has been touted in the press as an exceptional player simply because she qualified for a male team. Few noticed that the team was playing at the lowest competitive level in boys' hockey, and this kind of shortsightedness has colored the entire debate about sports integration.

Many people now assume that the best female athletes should be moving up to male events. What an insult to world-class athletes like runner Angella Issajenko, skier Laurie Graham and our Canadian Women's Field Hockey Team, who are every bit as skilled as their male counterparts! Should we dismiss these women as second-rate just because they can't outmuscle equally trained men?

No one disputes the notion more forcefully than female athletes. In most sports, the vast majority of girls want to play in an all-female environment where they can enroll at an early age and progress to the upper levels. They want to match their competitors in size and strength as well as dedication and mental acuity.

Integrated teams may meet girls' needs in a few sports, such as shooting, where a more muscular opponent cannot dominate competition. But in many others, integration would make females the losers. Each sport's promise for integration is best evaluated by its own governing body, not by ill-informed feminists.

Like it or not, male and female bodies do not perform identically. Medical evidence indicates that the differences are negligible until puberty, when girls gain a temporary edge in size and strength. But the situation reverses at about age 14. And if teen-age girls are to have the teams they deserve, we must nurture and protect the entire female stream.

If we allow girls like Justine Blainey to play on inferior male teams, how can we deny boys the chance to play on often-superior female teams? Last season, the O.W.H.A.'s male applicants included a 14-year-old boy who felt that the girls' program offered better opportunities than the boys'. But letting boys in creates a new problem: displacement of girls by more powerful players.

Integration will lead to exploitation of female athletes. Girls will be lured from top female teams by coaches of male teams who want sensationalized media coverage and increased funding (often allocated on a per capita basis). These girls will be recruited at puberty to help bring the male team a championship, and will then be discarded when biology overtakes them.

Meanwhile, the loss of girls from the female system will leave their former teammates with fewer opportunities. The defection of one or two players has been known to kill a team, and those that survive such blows will then face a shortage of money. Cost-slashing governments will likely decide to fund only one team per sport. Universities, now fending off requests for increased funding of women's teams, could well go the same route.

In Quebec, which has allowed integration since 1978, female sporting opportunities have not expanded. Only 35 girls' hockey teams exist, compared to 286 in Ontario; and almost 300 girls play on boys' teams, compared to 55 in Ontario.

If we really want more opportunities for female athletes, then let's start giving girls more funding, facilities, media coverage, corporate sponsorships and elite opportunities. And let's stop demeaning female teams with cheap talk about integration. We need not defeat men in head-to-head combat on the playing field to prove we're their equals.

Activities

1. With a partner, list the arguments each writer offers to support her position. Using the following criteria, evaluate which essay
   - offers the greatest number of arguments,
   - offers the best arguments,
   - presents its arguments in a way that convinces the reader most effectively.

2. In a journal entry, write your response to the two essays indicating which side of the issue you support.

3. With a partner, identify the thesis or main idea of each essay. Evaluate each thesis for the following:
   - how clear it is
   - whether it is phrased in a way that interests the reader
   - the effectiveness of its placement in the essay
   Share your evaluations with another partnership.

4. Write a letter to the Human Rights Board in your province in which you argue for or against the right of girls to play on a boys' team. Use facts provided in the essays to support the position you take.

5. Debate one of the following resolutions. Research may be necessary.
   - Be it resolved that ability and not gender should be the only criterion for gaining a position on a team.
   - Be it resolved that reporters of both sexes should receive equal access to locker room interviews after sporting events.

Kid's Games

Errol Black

ur games followed the cycle of seasons. In the early spring—that brief period when the heat of the sun wrecked the rinks and roads and turned vacant lots and fields into mud—we got out the marbles.

We played a number of games, but the most popular was played off the back of the school wall. It was a simple game. You'd throw your marble against the wall. Then the other player would throw his and try to get it as close to your marble as possible. The player who got his marble close enough to the other marble to span it—link the marbles with his thumb and middle finger—picked up both marbles.

The marbles were, for the most part, standardized—the glass marbles with some coloured swirls in them. But you also got "plumpers" (large marbles), ball bearings, wooden marbles, solid-coloured glass marbles, and occasionally exotic marbles, which some kid had received as a gift from relatives in some far-off place.

Because of this variation we had to fix exchange rates; i.e., establish relative values for the different marbles. For example, a "plumper" was worth two standard marbles, and two wooden marbles were the equivalent of one ball bearing. I don't recall exactly how the values were established, but I think it was based rather more on scarcity than the labour theory of value.

The game was addictive. Many evenings we played until our hands were so cold we couldn't extend them to make a span. When we lost our stock of standard marbles, we borrowed from other players, using our most prized marbles as collateral. As I recall, there were even a couple of kids who specialized in making loans—usually bigger kids. I'm still not sure what the attraction of the game was. It may have been the competition

and the pleasure of besting a rival. But it may also have been
a manifestation of the base instincts which motivate capitalist
accumulation.

When everything dried up, we put the marbles away and got
out our baseballs and bats. We played conventional games in
Rideau Park or on vacant corner lots. When we couldn't get
enough kids together to have a proper game, we played "tick".
This was a perverse game, because any time the bat made
contact with the ball the batter ran the bases. We soon learned
that the way to stay at bat was never to hit the ball into fair
territory. You fouled it over the head of the catcher or side-
swiped it so it went outside the base lines. The only time you
hit a fair ball was when the fielders attempted to defend against
the foul balls. To keep the game going we often had to impose a
rule restricting the skillful hitters to a maximum number of hits
for each time at bat.

We also played "poor-man's cricket" (also called "tin-can
cricket" and "can-i-can"). The game was played according to
cricket rules, but we used baseballs and bats and tin cans in
place of wickets. These games were dominated by the kids who
were shown the fundamentals of bowling and batting by their
fathers. The rest of us spent most of our time retrieving the ball
for the bowler.

I haven't seen this game played in Brandon for a long time,
but it's still played in other places. I was in Oshawa a couple
of years ago and happened to end up at a community club
windup. They gave out trophies for a number of inter-club
sports competitions, including tin-can cricket.

There was another game we played when there was just a few
of us around called "over-the-wire". At the time Manitoba
Telephone System had a number of overhead double lines of
heavy cable with braces tying them together. We'd have teams
on either side of the wire. The rules were baseball rules. The
player up to bat would throw the ball at the wire. If he missed
the wire three times in a row, he was out. If he hit the wire and
the ball wasn't caught by an opposing player it was a hit. Further
hits would advance the runners until you got a run.

This game had its share of quirks and risks. One of the
problems that plagued us was getting the ball wedged between

the double wire. When this happened we would throw rocks until a direct hit dislodged it and we could resume the game. The main risk was hitting the cars parked on the street. There weren't many, but there were some, and it could cost up to $20 to replace a windshield. As well, you could get injured. Some players liked to stand directly under the line and throw straight up at the bottom of the cable. If it hit, it would come straight back down. The kid trying to field it sometimes got the ball in the eye or off the forehead.

Kids couldn't play this game now even if they wanted to. The double lines have long since disappeared, either replaced by single lines or buried underground. But even if the lines were there, it wouldn't be a good game to play, because there are many more cars on the street and the cost of replacing windshields and doing body work is much higher than it was in our day.

In the fall we switched from games with baseballs to games with footballs (the kind they use in North American football). When there were enough kids around we got up a game of tackle football. It was rough, and sometimes when people had grudges, dirty stuff, but apart from bruises, scratches, split lips and loose teeth, there weren't many injuries. When there were just a few kids around we played yards—which involved kicking and throwing the ball back and forth until one team had advanced enough to get it over the goal line (which, in the park, meant getting it into the bushes at one end or the other of the circle).

When winter hit, the hockey gear came out and we played virtually non-stop until the spring. The rink in the East End had (and still has) two sheets of ice, which meant that we never had to give up the ice so that girls and little kids could skate. We were there most evenings and on Sunday afternoons. The rest of the time we were on the roads.

The nice thing about road hockey was that you could have a decent game with just about any number of players on a team— from one upwards. For goal posts we used lumps of snow, chunks of firewood or pieces of coal—and if you were really stuck there were usually a few horse buns around (in those days milk and bread deliveries were still made in horse-drawn sleighs). We preferred wood or coal, but there was a bit of a problem with using this stuff where we lived. There was a little old woman—Mrs. McKay—who used to come down our street on her way home. If we were using coal or wood, she would stop, pick them up and tuck them in her bag. We never said anything, we just replaced them with something else.

Sticks then were more durable than they are now. A good thing too, because we were lucky to get one new stick per winter. When they cracked, or broke, we patched them up with glue, nails, tin, wire and tape. One time an old fellow who lived next door to us gave me a stick he had in his back porch. It was a stick like none I'd ever seen before and none I've seen since. A one-piece job made out of fir. It was indestructible. But the blade didn't lie flat to the road. And it was heavy. When we were short sticks we made one of the goalies use it.

The games themselves were always exciting. We took the names of NHL stars. The goalies always wanted to be home-town hero, Turk Broda. There could only be one Broda, so the other was usually Terry Sawchuk. The rest of us were the Rocket, Gordie Howe, Ted Kennedy, Bill Juzda or one of the Bentley boys. We usually started out playing to ten. But when one of the teams got nine, the losing team would try to negotiate the score up to 15 or insist that it would be two games out of three. Sometimes we'd get up a game with a gang of kids a few blocks over. These were games we hated to lose. When we did lose, we invented excuses to explain it away, for example, "their goalie kept moving the goal post in to narrow the goal".

Today, road hockey is high-tech. The kids use real nets. They have $20 hockey sticks. And they use tennis balls instead of pucks. They don't have the finesse we did. Nor do they have the same stamina. All the games now seem to end at five o'clock. Some of our families used to eat at five, but we always made a point of playing on the streets where the kids ate at six.

We gave up the kid games when we hit Junior High School. This was when we got involved in organized sports—hockey and baseball—and play became more regimented and purposeful—less spontaneous. It was also about this time that we started to get interested in girls. We'd never paid much attention to them before, and we certainly never played any games with them. They played girls' games—hopscotch, skipping and games with rubber balls—in nice weather. And in the winter they just skated. I think it's the same now. I know when I go up to the rink, I don't see any girls on the hockey ice. And they don't seem to play road hockey. They now have a girl's game which is similar to hockey—ringette—but it's played mainly on indoor rinks.

I'm not sure what to make of this. Most adults—not all—look back on their childhoods with great fondness. And we always think our childhoods were "better"—tougher, more fun, etc.—than anyone else's. Like the farm kid who walked two miles [3.2 km] uphill to get to school and then walked two miles [3.2 km] uphill to get home again. Or the kid who lived in a part of the city so poor that the main form of recreation in the summer was trapping flies around the garbage cans in backlanes.

For us, games were a central part of our lives, especially the games we organized and played on our own. We really didn't have many alternatives. There was radio and reading (mainly comic books), but that was about it. The other thing I remember about these games is that everybody who showed up got to play; indeed, I remember some road hockey games when we had up to 15 kids on each side.

Kids today (at least kids who come from families where one or both of the parents are working on a regular basis) seem to have more alternatives than we did—T.V.s, V.C.R.s, Nintendo games, etc. Organized sports also start at a much earlier age than in my time. Now they get them started in hockey, soccer and baseball (T-ball and mush-ball) when they're five or six years old. Nevertheless, you still see kids playing their own games; in the streets, the park, vacant lots, and other places where they can get out from under adult authority and adult control and play just for the fun of it.

Somehow or other I find this reassuring.

Activities

1. With a partner, list all the games mentioned in this essay. Make a second list of games you have played that are not mentioned in the essay. Beside each game on your lists, indicate whether it is a sport or a game. Write a statement about the difference between the two categories and share it with other partnerships.

2. The author observes a few ways in which aspects of the games of his childhood have changed. Referring to a game you know has changed in recent years, write your thoughts about whether the changes have had a negative or positive effect.

3. Write a description of one game you played that other members of the class may not know about. Using your written work as reference, summarize the rules and procedures for playing the game to your classmates.

4. In a journal entry, explain why you believe that playing games is or is not an important part of growing up.

End of Unit Activities

1. Research biographical information about a famous athlete. Write an account of the individual to share with classmates. You might collect the biographies together in a book and give it a title, such as *Great Names in the World of Sports*.

2. Using a quotation about sports, athletics, or fitness, make a collage to display in the classroom.

3. In a group of three, brainstorm a list of figures of speech that, although associated with games and sports, are used to describe events in our daily lives. Your list might include examples such as "ballpark figure" and "tough sledding." Using one example from your list, make an oral report to the class about the relationship between sports and daily life.

4. Conduct a survey of the way people rate specific qualities of athletes associated with five different sports. For each sport, ask people to rate the qualities on a five-point scale (1 being the lowest; 5 the highest). Decide what qualities you want people to rate. They might include the following: honesty, daring, intelligence, courage. Report on the results of your survey to the class.

5. Debate one of the following resolutions:
   - Be it resolved that professional athletes are overpaid.
   - Be it resolved that performance-enhancing drugs are similar to other training and diet procedures and should be allowed.
   - Be it resolved that true sportsmanship can be developed through team sports only and not through single performance sports.
   - Be it resolved that all future disputes between nations should be resolved through athletic competition between the top athletes of these nations.

6. Write an essay on one of the following topics. Research may be necessary.
   - Participaction is or is not working in Canada.
   - The state of youth fitness in Canada.
   - The most obscure sport in the world today is....
   - Boxing and hunting should be banned as sports.

The Getting and Spending of Money

The world is too much with us; late and soon.
Getting and spending, we lay waste our
powers.

WILLIAM WORDSWORTH,
POET

Business, you know, may bring money, but
friendship hardly ever does.

JANE AUSTEN,
NOVELIST

To be clever enough to get all that money, one
must be stupid enough to want it.

G.K. CHESTERTON,
WRITER

I must say I hate money but it's the lack of it I
hate most.

KATHERINE MANSFIELD,
SHORT STORY WRITER

Young Money: Spending Power of Teens Has Rocketed

Lisa Grogan

anada's teenagers have big spending money in their pockets, possibly more than $3.5 billion a year, because two different needs in the economy have coincided.

Service businesses, short of low-cost help, are hiring more teenagers to flip hamburgers, pump gas and wait on tables. And more of the young people want the part-time work to buy themselves luxuries that are fast becoming essentials.

As the economy has roared ahead at close to full employment, businesses in many parts of the country have been competing fiercely for unskilled workers, driving up wages. Service operations (particularly in fast-foods and retailing) needed new pools of people willing to work for low wages. Teenagers and senior citizens have been filling the gaps.

Almost half of Canada's teenagers have taken jobs in the past few years, usually part-time, but in some cases full-time. (Many industries consider a 37.5 hour week full-time work.)

In a world of advertising targeted at affluent Yuppies, today's teenagers have not only rising expectations, but well-defined tastes. To pay for them, most have to work.

Many marketing experts say today's teens are sophisticated and worldly in comparison with past generations. One U.S. market researcher calls the current crop "the power children." They know what they want and how to get it.

Their wants range from fancy clothes, cars and video games to wrist watches, sports equipment and travel. The economic power of North America's teenage population has mushroomed as never before.

Francesca Derra, a 17-year-old at University Hill School in Vancouver, has worked an average 20–25 hours a week after school since she was 15.

"I was saving for a stereo," she says, "but my main goal now is to finance a six-month trip to Europe after I graduate, and then to pay for university."

Monica Barden, 19, a student at North Toronto Collegiate Institute, works part-time for a magazine. She says her friends, who work mainly in clothing shops, restaurants and video stores, are saving for travel and other large-ticket items.

Max Cleeveley, a 14-year-old at Martingrove Collegiate Institute in Metro Toronto, works part-time to save up for a car—either a Jeep or a Volkswagen Golf. "We're not just working so we can blow it every week," he explains.

One result of such ambitious spending patterns and the potential to develop brand loyalty early on has been a flurry of preliminary market research into how best to reach teenagers.

George Jackson, director of briefing and current analysis in the federal department of Employment & Immigration, says there is a direct link between falling unemployment and the rising percentages of working teenagers.

During the recession in 1981–82, teenagers were the first group to drop out of the labor force, and their numbers fell sharply. But since 1983, teenagers have been on the comeback, and they're entering the work force in droves.

In January [1989], according to Statistics Canada, the seasonally adjusted unemployment rate was 7.6%. The percentage of youths aged 15–24 with jobs had surged to a high of 62.9%, surpassing the previous record of 62.1% set last May [1988].

Jackson says this increase is more impressive than it looks, because the total population in that age group has fallen from a record 2.3 million in 1978 to 1.85 million in 1988.

Of the 1.4 million full-time high school students in Canada, 559,000 work part-time and another 69,000 claim to be looking for work. That means 44.4% of students hold down at least one job after school. Some have more than one.

Here, as in all industrial nations, the service sector is growing faster than manufacturing. Employment in Canada's service and producing industries rose by 2.6% in January [1989], but employment in the services sector alone shot ahead by 5.1%.

Most teenagers take jobs in restaurants, stores and supermarkets. And many of them work split-shifts, says Ray Ouimet, president of the Sportscene Restaurants Inc. chain in Montreal, which employs large numbers of teenagers.

"Salaries are primarily tip-driven," Ouimet says. "Above the hourly wage of $4.03 an hour, a good waiter is earning up to $125–$150 a day. That's very good money for anyone, plus, it's tax-free."

Ouimet says the tips guarantee a steady stream of would-be waiters, but he finds it more difficult to find dishwashers and potato peelers. Teenagers turn up their noses at such employment, which is mainly taken by new immigrants.

The problem is more acute in Toronto, where growth has been even faster. Fast-food chains and supermarkets, which have no-tipping policies, find it increasingly difficult to attract teenagers, so they are recruiting younger and younger workers.

One of the biggest employers of teenagers is fast food dispenser McDonald's Restaurants of Canada Ltd. A typical McDonald's teenage employee is Max Cleeveley, who works as a part-time cashier in an outlet near his Metro Toronto home. He says about 95% of the people employed in the outlet are high school students, and he figures at least 70% of his friends work.

Cleeveley's part-time starting wage is $4 an hour. It will be reviewed after four months, then every six months thereafter, and Cleeveley looks forward to raises of 25¢, 30¢ or 35¢ an hour.

The surge of young people in the labor force raises some troubling questions. How, for example, does this affect the teenagers' education? What are the long-term implications for the quality of the labor force? Are parents—and governments—sufficiently concerned about children working long hours?

To put it another way, are kids being encouraged to enter the adult world too early?

The increase in youth employment already worries the Ontario government. As in most other provinces, more than 30% of Ontario high school students drop out, and that number is likely to increase.

Ontario Premier David Peterson commissioned a study on the dropout issue last year [1988]. George Radwanski, who headed the commission, warns of a direct link between part-time work and the increasing number of high school dropouts.

"A heavy load of part-time work during the school year increases the likelihood of dropping out," he says.

The 15th hour of work is generally thought to be the dividing line. Any hours worked beyond that in a week make dropping out more likely. Statistics Canada says students in Grade 11 or lower work an average 11.7 hours a week, and the hours rise to 13.4 a week in the senior years.

Radwanski believes it is up to the high school system through "friendly persuasion" to make students and parents aware of the damage excessive part-time work can do to students' future prospects, both in terms of education and future employment.

He also accuses the business community of being "short-sighted" and "socially irresponsible" in giving students excessive part-time work. He suggests business should employ only students getting satisfactory marks.

To Radwanski (and others) the business community is myopic. It may be getting the low-skilled workers it needs now, but it is sabotaging the future labor force and thus the country's competitiveness. By employing young people in routine jobs, it is putting short-term needs ahead of the longer-term need to nurture a highly skilled labor force.

Many franchisees in the Harvey's Restaurants chain, a large employer of teenagers, provide time for study on certain shifts. Harvey's wants to convince the young employees there are career opportunities in the service field, explains Martin Peskin, vice-president of Harvey's, a division of Cara Operations Ltd.

At McDonald's, Roy Ellis, director of personnel and assistant vice-president, says the company monitors the hours of its teenage employees. He claims they are not allowed to work more than 15 hours a week to avoid conflict.

"Each student is working according to an availability schedule he or she supplies to us," he says. "Some students offer to work up to 30 hours a week, but we won't allow it."

Moreover, McDonald's holds family nights with parents to discuss their children's commitments, and rap sessions are organized regularly with employees to discuss concerns. Each year, every McDonald's restaurant awards one employee a $400 scholarship for continuing studies.

Employment & Immigration's Jackson has mixed reactions to the problem.

"High school teachers across the country are critical of students working part-time and not doing homework," he says, "but at least those kids who can handle it are getting some experience in the labor force and learning what it's like to hold down a job."

Linda Jones, a district career counsellor with the Vancouver School Board, is a proponent of part-time work. She says a job enables students to develop independence early and explore career opportunities. In some cases, average or below average students develop a sense of self-esteem they may not acquire through school.

Norman Ornes, principal of Vancouver Technical Secondary School, is also a believer in part-time work. Many of his students must work to supplement their family incomes, but he says he rarely sees one who cannot handle the pressures of both school and work.

While educators and economists complain that students are losing out on higher education, the lure of greater financial independence will continue to attract youngsters. Eventually, students will have to decide whether the short-term appeal of a steady pay cheque is worth sacrificing long-term goals.

One consolation for those concerned about child labor is that teenage workers will almost certainly be the first to lose their jobs as the economy slows down over the next year or so.

Activities

1. Because this essay was written in 1989, it includes factual information relevant to that year. With a partner, determine one piece of information in the essay that is not true today. Develop a class list of examples of "dated information" included in the essay.

2. With a partner, list the positive and negative effects of part-time jobs for teenagers identified in the article. Using the list as a reference, write your own defence or critique of part-time jobs for high school students.

3. List the reasons why teens work that are identified in the essay. Rank them in order of the most common reason to the least common reason. Compare your ranking to those prepared by two other students.

4. As a class, list the part-time jobs held by students in your class. Discuss your responses to each of the following statements:
   - Most part-time jobs for teens exploit the cheap labour of young people.
   - Part-time jobs for teens are society's way of indoctrinating young people into their roles as members of our consumer society.
   - Part-time jobs for teens do not really develop work skills in young people that will be useful in their adult lives.

5. Write a short essay explaining why you do or do not have a part-time job and how you feel it might affect your studies.

6. In a journal entry, describe your ideal part-time or summer job. You might mention details about working conditions, remuneration, and provision of training for the future.

7. With a partner, write and perform a dialogue on one of the following:
   - A parent and a teen discuss whether the teen should get a part-time job.
   - The personnel manager of one of the businesses mentioned in the essay interviews a teen applying for a first job.
   - A teen responds to a difficult customer at one of the businesses mentioned in the essay.

Brands Я Us: How Ads Reflect Our Consumer Society

Stephen Garey

yundai tells us that their cars make sense, Apple Computer offers us the power to be our best, and most of us don't believe a word of it. The fact is, when all is said and done, most people don't believe, don't remember, don't even notice, most advertising. This has always been so and always will be so. The vast majority of advertising is ineffective and inefficient.

And yet, there is a direct connection between a society's (or individual's) levels of exposure to advertising and the levels of consumption. How can this be? If advertising is inefficient, if 90 percent of all advertising is neither seen nor remembered by most people (according to surveys), if two minutes after being exposed to a particular message or brand I can no longer remember either the brand or the message, then where's the connection? How does something so banal and benign impact my consumption patterns and habits?

The message cited above for Hyundai automobiles ("Cars That Make Sense") has little or no effect either upon our personal lives or even Hyundai's sales overall. And we could say the same thing about thousands of other individual and isolated advertiser efforts. But the Hyundai advertising, combined with Apple Computer's advertising, combined with advertising for Tide detergent and Chivas Regal and RCA and Johnson's Floor Wax and the limited-time specials at your local department store or supermarket, has a very powerful collective effect indeed: it instructs us to Buy!

And it gives us, via lighthearted entertainment, permission to ignore the long-term consequences of our purchasing decisions by suggesting to us that we should not take any of this too seriously. (We shouldn't take a spilled glass of water too seriously, either. But a flood is a totally different matter.)

Advertising's real message, to buy and to buy ever more, to replace what we have rather than repair what we have, at one time served us well. When we were smaller in numbers, when we were still growing, still searching for a collective identity, when personal prosperity was touted as the primary reason for being alive, private property the only form of wealth, and when we were naive enough to believe it all, consumption and the ability to consume (choosing our livelihoods on the basis of whether or not it provided us with that ability!) was not only a way of life, it was a respectable one at that.

But we are no longer small in numbers. And we are no longer that naive. We can plainly see that advertising's collective power and our collective response to it has had, and continues to have, a profound and adverse effect upon our personal lives and upon the planet we share.

But pointing a finger at the advertising industry will change nothing. Wishing and hoping that the advertising industry will lose its innocence and suddenly leap into modern times in recognition of the situation we are all in is futile. And while the advertising industry is part and parcel of an industrial civilization now in decline, this doesn't mean we should expect the number of advertising messages and collective power of those messages to also decline in the very near future. If anything, it means we can expect an increase in the number of those messages. For the advertising industry, along with the main body of industrial society, is struggling for survival. It may be drowning, but it has not yet sunk. And in a last-ditch effort to save itself, it will flail about more wildly and make more noise than ever, as we might expect from any drowning individual.

No, what must change is us. What must change is how we see advertising in the context of the modern moment. We must recognize that its influence upon our lives and our well-being is in direct proportion to the amount of exposure in our lives, and that this exposure is an event unto itself, an experience separate from whether or not we respond to or believe individual messages.

High consumption has far more impact upon our environment than type of consumption. Buying much less and driving much less is better than just switching from plastic to paper or from "normal" unleaded to "super" unleaded. One of the first steps we must take towards consuming fewer goods is to consume less advertising.

Activities

1. With a partner, discuss what you think is the author's thesis or main point to be proved in this essay. Present your opinion to your classmates.

2. Conduct a survey to establish whether the author's assertion that most people don't remember the details of advertisements is valid. Use product sayings and logos from media and print commercials. Make sure that the product names are removed. See how many people in your class identify the product names for the samples. Summarize your findings to verify the accuracy or inaccuracy of the author's assertion.

3. In a journal entry, describe your favourite commercial. Indicate whether the commercial has made any impact on your consumer habits.

4. In a group of three, write a script for either a commercial advertising a product or a public service message. Prepare a videotape using your script and present it to the class. After viewing other student-prepared commercials, discuss with classmates which was the most effective.

5. Research information about the role advertising plays in our society. If possible, interview people who are employed directly and indirectly by the advertising industry. Learn some of the costs of advertising on television, radio, and in print. Find out how much is spent annually on advertising by one large Canadian organization. Write a report on your findings to present to the class.

6. Debate the following: Be it resolved that without advertising, Canada's economy would collapse.

A Touch of Humour

Capitalism Boiled Down

Stuart McLean

The Harvard Business School uses a teaching technique known as the case study method. Students at Harvard are presented with summaries of real business problems that real business executives have sweated over. Their assignment is to absorb the case study and propose solutions that might have worked in the real world. When they finish, they get to compare their ideas with what really happened.

You have just enrolled in the Stuart McLean School of Business. This is case one.

Ernie is a street vendor. He sells hotdogs from a wagon in downtown Toronto. He is probably the best hotdog salesman in the city. He may just be the best in the country. Like all good salesmen Ernie has a good feel for his product and he isn't shy to talk about it.

"The steamed hotdog was basically made famous in New York, and if you go down to New York City you'll find all of these hotdog vendors around Times Square, outside the Penn Station. And people come from all over the world to have a steamed hotdog. Damon Runyon made them famous in a series of stories when some of the Runyon crew such as Rusty, Charlie and Harry the Horse used to run down to Times Square to get a steamed dog. Everybody started saying, we have to have a steamed dog. You know, what we tell people here is that this is a classic steamed dog. Buy one and you can almost picture yourself in New York City. You're almost there. You've got this steamed dog with sauerkraut and red sauce. And red sauce looks wonderful on white sauerkraut. It's like blood on snow, and the whole hotdog takes off. You bite into the dog and think of the vendors on Times Square, the theatre district and you know you can take people there. It's great stuff."

Ernie is so good at what he does that there are a substantial number of people in Toronto who are eating more hotdogs than they know they should. I know this because I am one of those people. Ernie sells his hotdogs where I teach, on the campus of the Ryerson Polytechnical Institute. He turned up one autumn with his stainless-steel hotdog wagon, and never left. He stayed, in fact, all winter. His tenacity made an impression on a number of people at Ryerson, including two of my students, Tim Richardson and Dean Askin.

"I remember thinking how weird it was seeing a guy selling hotdogs outside in the middle of the winter. It was so cold sometimes, and you don't see too many street vendors in the middle of the winter, especially standing out there all day. But Ernie did it, he was there, he was there for us."

"It's true, he was the only vendor in a...well, in a forever block radius right throughout the cold weather. One day I saw him in the foyer taking five minutes to get warm, and then he went back out again, to sell more hotdogs. The man is remarkable. I don't know how he stood out there all winter in that cold, but he did, and people like him for it."

Ernie's stick-to-it-ness and delightful manner combined to win him a lot of customers. By the end of that first winter, his business, which had expanded steadily, was well established. By the time the weather warmed up that spring, he had a good thing going. Sure enough, it wasn't long after the snow melted that another vendor appeared and tried to move in on Ernie's territory.

Ernie is fifty-eight years old. We are going to call the competition the Young Guy. The Young Guy began setting up his cart every day right beside Ernie, and did his best to cut into Ernie's business.

The Young Guy lasted less than a week. Ernie blew him out of the water. You would go out at noon and see seven or eight people lined up in front of Ernie's wagon, and the Young Guy would be alone, clicking his hotdog tongs, trying in vain to attract business. One day he just didn't come back. Tip your hat to consumer loyalty and give round one to Ernie.

The second competitor showed up in the fall. But this time the competition was a little stiffer. A Greek restaurant owner named Chris set up his stall about a mustard squirt away from Ernie's wagon. Before long the gloves came off. Chris started a price war. He dropped the price of his dogs by twenty-five cents. Ernie consulted his financial backer, a man I know as Tony.

"We matched the price initially. OK, a quarter, all right, we can live with that. I think he went another dime lower but we let him. It just didn't attract the trade. I mean, all you have to do is taste the dogs. Like I say, you get what you pay for. It didn't work and he saw that it wasn't working so he brought his prices back up to par."

Give round two to Ernie. In round one he blew away the Young Guy. In round two, because of customer loyalty, he was able to hold the line on prices.

You might have forgiven Ernie if he had started to coast. He was firmly established, if you will excuse the expression, as top dog on the campus and had successfully turned away two assaults on his business. But it was at this point that Ernie displayed the brilliance that makes him one of the best hotdog salesmen in the country. Instead of resting on his laurels, he began to do exactly what the government says Canadian industry so often neglects. Ernie started to invest in R and D. He set out to improve his product.

"People think it's a simple product, but you have to find the right wiener for the particular area you're in. We've done that now, but we didn't start out with the same wiener we have today. The other thing is, you've got to match the bun. That took us almost five months before we found a bun that went with the wiener and was good for a steamed dog. Again, you have to look at the way you're going to do it. If you look at hotdogs, there are probably three major ways they're done. One is boiling, two is steaming and three is barbecuing. Boiling is a bad way of doing it because you take the flavour out of the wiener. Between the steaming and the barbecuing, steaming keeps the flavour in. Barbecuing is OK but it tends to dry out the wiener a little. But you've got to get a wiener for the technique you're using, and then you've got to get a bun to match the wiener."

Ernie settled on the Chicago 58 wiener and the egg bun with poppy seeds. But he didn't stop there. He also expanded his line of condiments. By his second spring, along with mustard and ketchup, he was offering Dijon mustard, sauerkraut, grated Cheddar cheese and a tub of home-made barbecue sauce from a secret family recipe. He would mix up the barbecue sauce over the weekend and had usually run out of it by Wednesday. As a crowning touch, Ernie offered all his customers a candy from a candy dish, just like the fanciest of restaurants.

In the face of this onslaught, Chris the Greek hung tough, but he was left scrambling. He went to the Chicago 58 wiener, too, but didn't add the poppy seeds to his buns. When Ernie added the grated Cheddar, Chris added Kraft slices. As to the price, he went beyond acknowledging that Ernie set the lead. He went as far as denying that he had ever started a price war.

"I never dropped my price. There was no competition. No, we've got the same price, me and Ernie. Same price. We never fight, we're friends, that's all. I go with the price he puts; if he goes up, I go up, too. If he goes down, I go down. I got the cheese because he put the cheese. I have to. He got the barbecue sauce, he got the hot mustard, he got everything. But I don't think I'm gonna add the candy, no."

Then one morning Chris the Greek upped the ante. He showed up with a gas barbecue on his wagon. Everyone was stunned. Including Ernie. Face it. A barbecue is classy. It not only smells good, it also has a certain rustic romance. Above all, it is good for business. For the first time ever, Chris started to attract customers.

Remember, this is a case study, right? Well, we have come to the test part. If you are Ernie, what do you do about the barbecue? Are your goodwill, your grated Cheddar, your poppy seed buns and your candy dish enough to pull you through this? Or do you go out and buy a barbecue for your wagon? If you stick with your steamer, are you going to see all your customers go up in smoke?

Do you dance with the girl what brung you?

Or do you buy a brand-new gas barbecue?

Before you read Ernie's strategy, you should pause here and decide on your answer. Here is Ernie's:

"Remember, if you are in a leadership position and the other people are following you, the day you follow them, that means they're in the leadership position. So for me to put a barbecue on my wagon means I would be following Chris. We won't do that. When we do something it has to be one step above him. We consider ourselves leaders."

Ernie held the line. He didn't buy the barbecue.

About a month after he made that decision, I went, at lunch, and sat on the grass and watched the two wagons for about half an hour. I went as an empirical scientist. I counted customers. In thirty minutes Ernie had thirty-three clients. Chris had twelve. As well as statistical information, just like any self-respecting sociologist, I collected anecdotal material. Lorri Neil and Laurie Gillies are students at Ryerson.

"It was about two weeks ago and it was a really nice day and some friends and I went to get a hotdog. There were about four people lined up at Ernie's wagon, but nobody was at the other guy's. So there were three of us and we looked over at the other guy and thought, well, too bad. We're gonna have Ernie dogs. So now there's seven people lined up at Ernie's, right? So we waited. It didn't matter. The other guy must have felt bad but it just didn't matter because we were willing to wait for Ernie dogs—steamed or not, who cares about a barbecue? I don't want a charcoal dog, anyway."

"I wouldn't go to the other guy at all. I mean, Ernie was there all the time. All winter. I'd feel disloyal if I went to the other guy. And it may sound silly over a stupid hotdog, but I'd go to Ernie over anybody else."

Ernie's continuing strong market position can be explained in a variety of ways. First, barbecue or no barbecue, there is much about Ernie's wagon to recommend it. He has the grated *Cheddar* cheese, the *poppy* seed buns, the *home-made* chili sauce and the *complimentary* candy. All things considered, it could be argued that he has a superior product. But it goes beyond that. The question of reliability has to be considered. Ernie showed up all winter. No one else was prepared to stand on the sidewalk in January, and people feel that sort of perseverance deserves to be rewarded. Finally there is the matter of service. Chris does a workmanlike job of selling hotdogs. He serves them up with competence. Ernie, however, has style. He has created a world. A world of steam and secret barbecue sauce, peopled by a fraternity of regulars who come back every day to buy their lunch from the world's greatest hotdog salesman. It's a world Ernie says he loves.

"What can I tell you? There's a lot of nice people in my world. We all meet around the central theme of what's new with hotdogs [Ernie laughs]. And so we always have to think of another story about a hotdog, and we come around one way or another. It's fun because there's no structure to it. We get all sorts of people around here and we can always kid them a bit. Some things they believe and some they don't. We're the magic deli of hotdogs, that's what we are."

No one really knows who Ernie is. He is a bit of a mystery. Tony, his boss, says he showed up one day wearing a suit and carrying a briefcase and asked him for a job. At first Tony thought he was a city inspector and was a little leery of hiring him. Now he wishes he had ten other guys like him. He looks like an ex-fighter or a stevedore, or someone who spent time with the French Foreign Legion. I know that Ernie is not his real name. It's a nickname one of the students gave him. He tells me that he used to sell semiconductor computer parts for some multinational corporation. He probably did. Ernie could sell anything.

Activities

1. With a partner, identify the three most important factors that you feel are responsible for Ernie's success. Be prepared to report your opinions to the class and defend them.

2. With a partner, evaluate the tone of this essay. What words and phrases help to develop the tone? Identify personal qualities that you think would describe the author. What words and phrases give you that impression? Be prepared to report your ideas to the class.

3. In a group of three, develop a description of a food vending business to put Ernie's hot-dog stand out of business. Work out a plan of operation that includes objectives, schedules, costs, and selling strategies to submit to the Stuart McLean School of Business.

4. In a journal entry, explain whether you would prefer to start and run your own business or work for someone else.

Shoppers' Heaven

Michael Salter

ostwar North America has invented no instrument more fiendishly clever at parting us from our money than the shopping mall. Take a look at the pages that follow. The modern mall is a village square, a Disneyland for adults and Aladdin's treasure cave all rolled into one. Enter those portals and prepare to surrender. Give in to your desires, lay down your credit cards, immerse yourself in the material world. It's a mindless, one-dimensional, highly pleasurable experience. Watch people walking out of the mall after several hours of shopping: They stop for a moment, blinking in the light. Where did they put the car? Why did they buy all this stuff? What happened in there, anyway?

Whatever it was, it didn't happen by accident. It was an experience carefully engineered by developers, retailers, store designers, architects and interior landscapers. A veritable horde of shopping-centre professionals have spent decades fine-tuning what they now call the "retail drama," a stage play of concrete, marble, glass and goods that's designed to make you buy more stuff than you ever knew you wanted.

Industry insiders speak reverently about the pioneers and innovators who, for better or worse, helped make the mall what it is today. They tell of brothers A. B. and D. E. Bennett, who broke ground for Toronto's first centres in the early 1950s. There's Victor Gruen, the Austrian-American architect who designed North America's first enclosed shopping centre in icy Minneapolis. Gruen worked closely with Neil Wood, the former president of Cadillac Fairview, who was the real brain behind the development of Toronto's famous Eaton Centre, probably the continent's most profitable mall.

Charles Tabachnick, president of Cambridge Leaseholds Ltd., specialized in malling midsized Canadian cities, where larger developers had feared to tread. Charles "Chunky" Woodward won the West with a string of malls across British Columbia and Alberta. And who does not know the Ghermezian brothers? These reclusive Iranian expatriates built the vast West Edmonton Mall, their vision of what North America should really look like.

The first shopping centres of the 1950s were strictly functional, creatures of the automobile and urban sprawl. They were "strip" centres, a long line of stores with lots of free parking. It sounds simple, but easy parking was the key to the mall's triumph over street shopping. Then came enclosed centres, which provided protection from nature and made it pleasant to browse.

Eberhard Zeidler, who designed the Toronto Eaton Centre, once said that architecture operates "by a kind of informed intuition, an emotional understanding of structure and social necessity." By the 1970s developers realized that their malls, already about the best income-producing real estate on the planet, could do even better by providing the sense of place that the suburbs lacked. They began talking about bringing the downtown's "streetscape" inside the mall; about promoting the mall itself as a "destination," not just a collection of stores. Developers started implanting the fiction that the shopping centre, a profit-making business, was a centre of genuine community activity. (People who try handing out "Stop the Arms Race" buttons to Saturday shoppers quickly discover this is not the case.) Malls sprouted trees, bushes, fountains, ponds, streams, benches, skylights, walkways, food courts, movie theatres, services and, lately, indoor amusement parks. Developers learned that the ambience of the mall itself strongly influenced the decision to buy. They coined new buzzwords: the shopping "environment," the shopping "experience," "event" shopping. And they added more events: fashion shows, charity ticket sales, telethons, petting zoos and visiting dee-jays, all designed to keep consumers coming back, to encourage them to forge a lasting bond with "their" centre.

The developers' biggest concern today is perfecting the art of the mix, making sure the mall has the right stores to appeal to local consumers. In the early days, developers simply copied the selling-everything-to-everybody format of the department

stores, renting space to a wide variety of retailers along the mall
in no particular sequence. Gradually, the emphasis switched to
higher-margin fashions and portable items that lend themselves
to impulse buys. The transformation is now complete. The big
indoor regional malls are called "fashion regionals," with most
of the stores devoted to women's, men's and children's fashion,
accessories, shoes and jewelry. And that transition accounts for
one of life's mysteries: that as malls get bigger and bigger, the
selection of what you can buy in them shrinks.

The mall of the late 20th century is part consumer heaven,
part monster, eating up time, money and land that could
probably be put to better use. Each age builds its own
monuments; like it or not, the shopping mall is our cathedral.

The centre court is the focal point of the entire shopping
centre, the area toward which shoppers are drawn like bees to
nectar. Developers spend big bucks here to create just the right
mood and tone. It's a better-than-real town centre, paved with
marble, free of cars, wide and open like a classical forum, rising
three or four stories to a lofty skylight. A fountain or pool is
always popular with snowbound Canadians. A central tower,
often with a clock and elevator to the second floor, is another
common flourish, reminiscent of the town halls of yester-year.
The open area is used for events—everything from fashion
shows to petting zoos.

All the best shops are clustered near centre court. This is
where developers unleash their retail thunder, the "prime mix"—
shops such as Lipton's, Mappins, Harry Rosen and Holt Renfrew.
The most exclusive stores are on the second level near centre
court, allowing their patrons to gaze down on the plebeians
below. Be warned: The centre mall is the place of least resistance.

Just inside the entrance, the developer puts "destination"
shops, which offer goods and services that don't rely on
browsing for sales. You'll find a bank or trust company, dentist,
dry cleaner, hair stylist, key cutter, shoe repair shop, possibly a
sit-down restaurant.

The trend in the 1980s has been to provide more and better
services. But you won't find appliance repairs, a seamstress or
a tailor. Unless the service is part of a chain or franchise, it often
can't survive the high rents of the mall. In the '90s, look for

day-care centres, doctors' offices and more financial services, including planners, and real estate and insurance agents.

The all-important department store "anchors" one or both ends of the regional shopping centre. Without an anchor, the mall simply doesn't get built. Because of their clout, anchors pay minimal rent and few common costs. The cheap ride

the department stores get means they don't feel the same performance pressure the specialty chains do. That's why they often look slightly rundown and old-fashioned.

The anchors have been losing market share for years, but they still draw the crowds that shop the specialty shops along the "spine" of the mall. The specialty stores pay for the anchor's free ride through higher costs. In Canada, the anchors have disproportionate power because of their small numbers. The major national chains are Eaton's, Sears, The Bay, Simpsons, Kmart and Woolco, while regional anchors include Ogilvy's, Robinson's and Woodward's.

The largest malls are adding permanent amusement areas for boomers and their kids. They draw inspiration from the West Edmonton Mall, which devotes 1.4 million [130 000 m²] of its 5.2 million square feet [480 000 m²] to rides and amusements. Les Galeries de la Capitale in Quebec City recently opened a 160,000-square-foot [15 000-m²] "leisure component," including a skating rink, a suspended roller coaster and a minia-ture golf course, while Toronto's Woodbine Centre has 45,000 square feet [4 200 m²] of kiddie rides. These areas are popular for children's birthday parties. One of the latest futuristic toys is a complex piece of technology called an interactive video wall—stand in front of it, wave your arms and make computer music and images. It'll be coming to a mall near you, soon.

Mall merchandise tends to carry sky-high price tags because the merchants pay sky-high rents. Mall developers try to protect themselves from inflation. They charge retailers either a minimum rent—averaging about $50 per square foot [$540/m²] in the better regionals—or 6% to 8% of their gross sales, whichever is greater. Once a retailer is paying percentage rent, the developer's take goes up with consumer prices.

Retailers' costs don't end there; they also pay "common area costs" of about $10 to $15 per square foot [$110 to $160/m²]. Common costs include everything from snow removal and realty taxes to cleaning, utility bills, promotion costs and structural maintenance. Essentially, the developer passes on most of the cost of running and maintaining the mall to the retailers, who pass it on to you.

The stage managers of the retail drama are the mall and promotion experts. While the mall manager collects rents and enforces the shopping centre's stringent rules on store cleanli-ness, punctual openings and closings and other matters, the promotion manager dispenses the ad and promo budget, which averages $1 million or more per year at a big regional mall. The Toronto Eaton Centre has a mega-budget of about $2.5 million.

The promotion manager's chief task is encouraging belief in the fiction that the mall, a privately owned concern, somehow "belongs" to the community. He or she must organize and promote an endless series of crowd-pleasing seasonal sales and special events: the January clearance sale; Valentine's Day; Easter; the spring fashion show; Mother's Day; Father's Day; summer clearance; back-to-school; and the fall fashion show. These sales are interspersed with periodic community events such as charity ticket sales, telethons, visiting radio dee-jays and car shows.

Woe to the promotion manager who doesn't ace the Christmas blowout. Preparing for the country's annual spending orgy consumes one-third of the yearly promo budget. The cost to buy, rent, install and take down Christmas decorations, including a Santa's Village, is more than $100,000. Ads cost extra.

Washrooms and lockers are unsightly and take up space that could otherwise be rented. In downtown shopping malls, these conveniences attract the homeless, who store their belongings in the lockers and bathe in the bathroom sinks—not the sort of behavior you want in the mall. That's why lockers and washrooms in malls are so few and far between. The rule of thumb is that when you need a washroom, it is always located at the other end of the mall from where you're standing. If you are accompanied by a small child and hope to find a changing table there, forget it.

Whether you're in Sarnia or Saskatoon, Lethbridge or London, chances are that you'll see the same shops. A handful of big specialty chains—most of them based in Toronto and Montreal—dominate fashion retailing in malls. Why? Because the chains have the financial clout, based on huge sales and volume buying, to survive high mall rents.

To squeeze every drop of profit from their expensive space, retailers are making their stores as small and efficient as possible by concentrating on the most popular styles and sizes. That's why your chances of seeing something unusual or getting small- or large-sized items at regular stores are disappearing.

Developers say they want variety, but what they really crave is proven performance. In fact, in return for a berth in a profitable centre, developers often force retailers to open stores in their second-string malls. No wonder small, independent retailers rarely get a good mall location.

Leasing agents are behind-the-scenes power brokers who work both sides of the street; they find mall space for retailers and help developers fill vacancies. Three leasing companies representing more than 150 chains dominate the mall-renting business in Canada. On cue, they can fill any shopping centre with tenants, making the developer sleep easy.

Movies and malls go together like popcorn and pop. For the developer, having theatres at the mall improves the image of the shopping centre as a destination, a place to go for many reasons, not only shopping. The movie exhibitor benefits by having free parking for his or her patrons and a warm, dry place where they can line up for tickets. Movie theatres in malls took off after Cineplex Odeon Corp. popularized the multiscreen format in the early 1980s.

Big malls usually contract for a security force of more than a dozen people, operating in shifts. Their chief tasks are to prevent loitering, combat shoplifting and the destruction of plants, and generally discourage non-spending activities.

King of the mall is Toronto's Dylex Ltd. It has 1,300 stores under 15 names—different stores to appeal to different age groups and income levels. Dylex's women's and men's clothing stores account for 10% of Canadian apparel sales. Big Steel Man sells cheap, fashionable clothing for young guys; Tip Top specializes in reasonably priced suits; Harry Rosen caters to the high-spending professional. Young women watching their dollars shop for fashion at Fairweather, B. H. Emporium or Suzy Shier. Women over 30 are supposed to shop at Town & Country and Braemar.

The chains divide up the market and charge accordingly. Peoples Jewellers runs 188 Peoples stores selling medium-priced jewelry, while its 81 Mappins stores sell more expensive baubles. Montreal-based Reitmans has 600 stores under four names, including Reitmans (low-ticket, low fashion), Smart Set (trendier) and Pennington's, which dominates the large-size women's clothing market with 102 Pennington's (oversized and cheap) and Liz Porter (oversized and pricier). The Grafton Group runs various men's wear chains (Jack Fraser, Elks), women's wear (Loft and Sideffects), plus the shoe and clothing sections at Woolco.

Developers know that the longer you stay, the more you'll spend. So they make sure you're not going to cut short your shopping trip just because you're hungry. Snacks at the food court are meant to deliver large amounts of fats and sugar to revive your flagging energy for more shopping. The food circus is never large or comfortable enough to encourage lingering. The average sitting time is less than half an hour; after that you're supposed to give up your seat to the people glaring at you as they wait for you to finish.

You won't find exotic edibles here. The most popular fare: burgers, fries, pizza, fried chicken, Chinese. The latest fads are frozen yogurt, cinnamon buns and chemically flavored popcorn. Considering the quality, prices are high. Food court retailers pay top dollar, up to $200 per square foot [$2,150/m²] annually in rent and maintenance costs, but their sales often reach $1,000 per square foot [$10,800/m²].

The stores near the food court are supposed to attract your attention as you sit munching and planning your next stop. They sell inexpensive impulse items such as gifts and lottery tickets.

Hordes of teenagers just hanging out are the unavoidable result of building malls in the suburbs, where teenagers often have nowhere else to go. They range from benign gaggles of giggling girls or prematurely macho guys to the menacing gangs of punks who "swarm" other kids and force them to give up their cash or leather jackets. Mall managers refer to all non-spending teenagers as "the youth problem." There's no solution, only an endless game of cat and mouse as security staff shuffle the loiterers off the premises—or at least away from the pricier stores.

Service is terrible at most department stores because top management has responded to shrinking market share (read: customer dissatisfaction) by cutting staff, causing yet more frustration. It's better at specialty stores, which can afford to have more bodies on the floor. Retailers have made massive investments in electronic cash registers and computerized inventory control systems, but they've found no mechanical substitute for a well-informed, courteous salesperson.

And with fewer young people coming into the labor force, cheap help is getting harder to find. Increasingly, seniors will staff the cash. Watch for more grey-haired hamburger-flippers.

Free parking for several thousand cars is the big drawing card of the suburban mall. The parking lot typically occupies 80% of the mall's total land area. The parking lot may look like an asphalt desert, but its size means there's plenty of space, except on weekends, of course.

Like casinos, shopping malls lack outside windows, the better to make you forget the time or the weather outside. Control is the name of the game. Malls are heated in winter and air-cooled in summer. It never snows, never rains. Malls have very few entrances and exits. Except for department stores, most stores can be entered only from the interior of the mall, ensuring that shoppers walk by as many stores as possible in their search for an exit.

A walk along the centre alley or "spine" is meant to excite shoppers into a state of spending readiness. The aisles in the mall are wide enough to allow you to see the store fronts clearly, but narrow enough so that when it's crowded, you feel slightly hurried and harried. Up and down the spine the developer puts medium-priced stores, clustering fashion, shoe and accessory stores by age suitability, style and "price point." Scattered among all that fashion are stores that round out the mix, including bed-and-bath stores, kitchen shops, electronics stores and even a bookstore.

How will the mall of the future look? Well, for one thing, it's unlikely to be surrounded by a giant parking lot. All that empty space means unrealized profit for developers. As the suburbs fill up, mall owners will build underground lots and parking garages, freeing up space for hotels, office towers and, yes, condominiums around the shopping centre. If you can't shop where you live, you'll be able to live where you shop.

As regional malls get bigger and the population ages, malls will follow the lead of West Edmonton Mall and provide patrons with motorized golf carts to do their shopping. And if trends here follow those in the United States, then we're in for mall walkathons and even mall marriage ceremonies.

Activities

1. With a partner, list the positive aspects of shopping malls described in the essay. Make a second list of aspects the author mentions that might be considered negative. Decide whether the author's attitude toward malls is more positive than negative. Share your decision with the class and be prepared to defend it.

2. Write a journal entry describing what you feel are the most positive and negative aspects of shopping malls. Explain why you do or do not like spending your free time in a mall.

3. With a partner,
   a) take photographs of a shopping mall in your community and prepare a poster that illustrates ways in which your community mall does or does not exhibit characteristics of the malls described in the essay

   OR

   b) look at the photographs that accompany this essay. Decide whether they effectively illustrate the points made in the essay. As the editor of this textbook, imagine that you need to
   · drop one of the photos because of space constraints,
   · add a photo to the layout.
   Decide which photo you would drop; then decide what photo idea would make an interesting addition to the ones featured. Share your conclusions with other partnerships.

4. Prepare a photo essay on a theme of your own choosing. Some possibilities might be special interest stores, community parks, street lighting, your school, or a hobby. Display your photo essay for classmates to view.

5. Interview one merchant who has a store in a mall and one merchant whose store is not part of a mall. Ask questions that will reveal information about the advantage of having a business in a street front store or in a mall. Summarize your findings in a report. You might conclude the report by indicating where you would choose to locate a business if you were to open one.

Canadian Dreamer

Catherine Collins

'm expansionistic in my thinking, I'm acquisitive and inquisitive, and I like to succeed," says Martin Connell, and you believe it. Even corralled into an easy chair in his corner office at Conwest Exploration Company Limited in Toronto, the chairperson's lanky frame and lean bearded face betray his intensity. Eyes warm and direct, he gets straight to the point, then chases it with a smile. "I *am* fundamentally ambitious."

Fundamentally, he is—like every other captain of industry. But where Martin Connell differs is in passionately wanting *others* to expand, succeed and be ambitious too. Since 1983, the 50-year-old millionaire has fanned the flames of hundreds of tiny entrepreneurial efforts through The Calmeadow Foundation, the private, nonprofit organization he created to lend money to the working poor, be they Bolivian bicycle porters or Cree basketweavers. Endowed with $1.3 million of Connell's personal fortune and his belief in the universal right to credit, Calmeadow launches the hopes and chances of impoverished entrepreneurs.

Helping developing people help themselves is not, of course, a new idea. Nor is the notion of providing loans to finance their small, bootstrap initiatives—or microenterprises as they have come to be called. For 15 years the Grameen Bank in Bangladesh, whose founder is often cited as being the father of the microenterprise credit movement, has been doing just that, as have a number of major development agencies, such as Accion International in the United States. What is remarkable about Connell's Calmeadow is not so much how it is helping others, but who is helping it. The corporate sector, traditionally tightfisted when it comes to development aid, has thrown its weight, respect and funding behind Connell's dream, because he's not just doing good, he's doing business.

"If we can enhance people's capacity to be more self-reliant, then everybody wins," he says, using words practical enough to win any corporate heart but with an idealist's shine in his eyes. "The donors see the payoff for their investment, the borrowers get access to something they could never otherwise have, which improves their sense of worth. And the payoff for *us* is the dignity that flows from their self-reliance."

Practical idealism shines not only in Connell's eyes and Calmeadow's work but in his mission as chairperson of Imagine, the Canadian Centre for Philanthropy's national campaign to boost the spirit of giving. Two and a half years into the campaign [in 1991], which takes him from coast to coast, speaking to corporations and individuals alike, he champions it not as a bid for charity but, like Calmeadow, as a mobilizer of human resources and initiative.

"I like words like 'venture capital' and 'merchant banking,' " he says energetically, "but stick the word 'social' in front of them. I live in a world where there are a *tremendous* number of people who are denied their dreams, oftentimes for nothing more complex than having no access to a very small amount of capital. I think of myself much more as a social entrepreneur than a philanthropist."

Think of this, then, not as the story of a charitable man but of a man for whom money is both an end and a means, a capitalist with a conscience, a businessperson leading peers toward tomorrow, just slightly ahead of his time.

Daylight pours into the Calmeadow boardroom and falls like a blessing on the management committee of the First Peoples' Fund. A lending program under the aegis of Calmeadow staff, it is steered largely by native Canadians like Shelle Brant of Tyendinaga, Ont., recently appointed the fund's manager. She's trying to prop up an unwieldy map of Canada and calls on her boss, Martin Connell, to assist. As he stands someone cracks, "He's your Vanna White," and the group shares a laugh at the thought of Connell, in shirt and tie, spinning the Wheel of Fortune.

It wasn't luck, however, but hard work that brought Calmeadow to this table. Four years ago Connell was inspired by the spirit of enterprise quietly percolating throughout

Wikwemikong Reserve on Ontario's Manitoulin Island. Though lacking collateral and any chance of credit, many band members were nonetheless running tiny informal businesses—such as a living-room pool hall and home-based native crafts—on nothing but sweat and ingenuity. He and his small Calmeadow staff, having explored the lending idea with the Grameen Bank and Accion, invited the band to start a community borrowing program. Founded on the principle of trust and self-honour, four to six of these small-scale entrepreneurs formed a borrowers' group, with Calmeadow guaranteeing the credit granted by the local bank. In exchange for receiving modest loans at commercial interest rates, each of the entrepreneurs assumed responsibility for repaying not only his or her debt but the rest of the group's, should anyone default. With the onus on them to manage their own business affairs (further credit is withheld until group debts are paid), the native borrowers got their first taste of financial independence.

Calmeadow's infusion of capital was like rain to a parched seedling. Microenterprise blossomed on the Wikwemikong Reserve, then on other Ontario reserves and is now flourishing across the country in the form of the First Peoples' Fund, as Shelle Brant graphically reports with the coloured pins clustered on her map. Over the next three to five years, about 70 native communities are expected to set up and run their own borrowers' circles, a goal that delights Randy Kapashesit, the alternate chair of the management committee. Director and chief of Mocreebec First Nation on Moose Factory Island, Ont., he says "the borrower's circle is like an artificial family, and for natives the family clan is the most fundamental organization. Self-sufficiency is something many of us once had and have been struggling to regain. I like the vision of First Peoples' Fund—for all of us."

Business likes the vision too. Calgary's Kahanoff Foundation and 40 other foundations and corporations have contributed $2.5 million in operating funds to the project, and all the major chartered banks have agreed to lend money to the communities through their local branches on the condition that each community guarantees 25 percent of the total line of credit, Calmeadow guarantees 50 percent and the bank takes

25 percent of the risk, charging commercial rates plus an extra 1.5 percent. So appealing is the goal of self-reliance for the disadvantaged that CCEC Credit Union in Vancouver and the Royal Bank in Lockeport, N.S., have linked up with Calmeadow and The Kahanoff Foundation this year [1991] to bring the idea of the borrowers' circle to nonnative communities.

"Business appreciates that money gets recycled," explains Connell, back in his own light-filled office, which opens onto an Oriental garden—and *real* air (such as it is in downtown Toronto). "It's not like a grant, where it gets dropped into the void. It comes back, it gets re-lent, it keeps on giving. And that's compatible with the corporate view."

Connell's pedigree is compatible too. Calmeadow's chairperson comes with the usual silver-spoon credentials— born into Toronto wealth and the Conwest mining dynasty, groomed for succession by his prospector grandfather, Frederick Connell, and crowned young ruler of the family fortune at 33. He is Establishment, and business likes that. "Calmeadow's great advantage over other nongovernmental organizations is that it's headed by someone who has visibility, influence and accessibility to money," says Nigel Martin, former executive director of the Canadian Council of International Cooperation, a coalition of national volunteer organizations that support Third World activities. "That opens doors."

But Connell's financial savvy, whether inherited or learned, gives him a greater edge than any old-boy legacy. His father-in-law, Cedric Haynes, former president of Crush International Limited and a veteran volunteer of the Canadian Executive Service Overseas (CESO), has seen first-hand why Connell makes a difference. "Many of these organizations have the right spirit to help people, and they do a good job," says Haynes. "But so often there's not the marketing analysis that goes into whatever Martin does. He's very methodical, developing his contacts, not rushing things too much—the way he's working now on this bank in Bolivia."

Methodical as he may be, Connell cannot repress his zeal over Banco Solidarios (Banco Sol, for short), a three-year dream in the realization. "In Bolivia, we've been working with a nonprofit lending organization called PRODEM, which now has 15,000 clients—the average loan is $175—all operating in what is euphemistically known as the informal sector" (one-owner businesses or family-owned enterprises, home-based and involved in everything from vending fruit to recycling bedsprings), he says. "Back in late '87 we started talking to prodem about converting it into an actual bank, and," adds Connell, half-delighted, half-disbelieving, "it looks like it will open this year."

With support from Calmeadow ($250,000 in equity), the Canadian International Development Agency (CIDA), Accion and Bolivian investors, Connell says Banco Sol has the potential to open financial doors for a quarter-million impoverished people. Pragmatically and philosophically, this is the kind of deal that best suits Connell. "I am probably *more* businesslike now than I was five years ago in my approach to Calmeadow. I mean, to think in terms of transforming an institution into a bank is an entrepreneurial gesture, and seeing myself as an entrepreneur who does these things is very compelling. I guess it's more consistent with my true nature."

Martin Connell's true nature is not an easy thing to define, least of all for Martin Connell, who shifts uneasily in his chair when conversation trespasses on his private life. On a surface reading, you see a smart, stylish go-getter who hustled through his twenties, marrying right out of Montreal's McGill University, fathering four children, climbing the Conwest ladder, investing on the side in restaurants and bars, divorcing and becoming chief executive officer and president by the tender age of 33. What caused such a man, not even at his corporate prime, to relinquish the seat of power to serve humankind better?

The temptation is to search for that pivotal moment when a life divides into before and after. But the truth is, the flowering of Connell's social conscience was a long, slow, sometimes painful, sometimes joyful evolution.

"Early on—I was an only child—I remember going to school and feeling there was something wrong with this picture," he says suddenly. "There were literally hundreds of millions of people out there living on the edge, and here I was, living the way I was, not because of any brains but pure blind luck. It *always* bothered me."

In many ways, however, Connell was a kid like any other—
"you know, searching for identity," says his boyhood chum Bill
Moore, assistant comptroller of Marathon Realty Company in
Toronto. The pair went through grade school together, and
although they chose different Toronto high schools, stayed in
touch during their teens. "I saw him on weekends when we
couldn't get dates," says Moore, "which was most of the time."

In other words, an ordinary boy, raised with the
extraordinary pressures of privilege. "There was a free spirit
there that he had to keep in check," says Moore. Friends allude
to tension between Connell and his father, John, who'd been
a Second World War fighter pilot and prisoner of war; the
pressure of living up to the love and example of his grandfather;
a family power struggle as he proved his salt at Conwest,
wresting equity control from his first cousin; the sadness of
divorce.

"Martin is innately kind, but his own problems gave him a
great deal of empathy for other people," says David Peterson,
former premier of Ontario, who became fast friends with
Connell on a rafting expedition down an Idaho river, when they
were in their twenties. At that time Connell had no grand
scheme to help the world. He did volunteer work for the
Salvation Army (a tradition begun by his father) and thought
about social inequity. But then, as now, says Peterson, "Martin
was a style-setter, not a missionary."

Like most of us in our younger years, Connell focussed
mainly on *his* life—his kids, his job, his money, his
opportunities. Life was fast and glamorous, deal-making at
Conwest by day and style-setting at his restaurants by night. A
catalyst even then, Connell financed partner Tom Kristenbrun,
now president of Chrysalis Restaurant Enterprises Inc., together
transforming many of Toronto's dowdy beverage rooms into
fashionable pubs. But none was what Kristenbrun would call a
gamble. "The risks he took with me were insignificant."

But they did reflect a restlessness, a free spirit kept in check.
Connell's inner search intensified when the sudden death of a
young daughter brought real heartache and introspection. By his
mid-thirties, Connell found himself in a rather premature
midlife crisis. "So I *did* take stock and reevaluate, and I

concluded that there were other things I could be doing that would be just as interesting and a little less—" he hesitates, wondering perhaps whether to supply the word "self-centred," and decides against it—"a little more involved with helping others."

Such was his state of mind when in early '79 he had what he calls the serendipitous encounter with his wife-to-be on a plane ride to Toronto. Linda Haynes, now 43, doesn't recall his confusion, just the compassion of a man who had accomplished his material goals and was ready to do more—just like her father, Cedric, whom she had visited only the month before in El Salvador. As if ordained, their interests and futures dovetailed.

That year Connell gave up the reins of Conwest's active management (though he remains keenly involved as chairperson), met a kindred spirit in Cedric Haynes and married a soulmate in his daughter. "It was wonderful for Martin to have my father to talk to," says Linda, a warm candid woman who quit a career as a TV producer to have two children, now nine and five, and be part-time mother to Connell's three from his previous marriage. "He really needed the reinforcement, because a lot of his business peers thought he was making a mistake."

It was Haynes' Third World work with CESO, putting his corporate skills into charitable practice, that pointed the way for Connell. "Ced had the practical experience, and I had some wacko dreams and schemes, so it was a good mix," says Connell, laughingly recalling that he was so inspired by Haynes that he immediately signed up to be a CESO recruit. "But I never got any calls!"

He did get a second father in Cedric Haynes, 78, who talks easily and lovingly from his winter home in Redington Shores, Fla., about the thoughtfulness that marks all of Connell's dealings. "I remember walking with him in our garden, and Martin approached me in the old-fashioned way and asked for Linda's hand in marriage. Of course it was up to Linda. But I thought that was something a little different for a modern-day businessman."

So did Linda, and a good thing too, for it was shortly after their wedding, cruising down the Nile in February 1980, that

Connell's vague yearnings to right humanity's wrongs were galvanized. "I was reading a book by Richard Critchfield, *A Day in the Life of an Egyptian Peasant*, and thought it ironic that here I was sitting on a luxury cruise boat on the Nile, dropping in on the historic sites by minivan, while all along the shoreline people were subsisting as they basically had since pre-biblical times, exactly as this book was telling me. It was a jarring contradiction." When he got home he contacted the volunteer agencies Inter Pares and Canadian Save the Children, then, that fall, he went with Linda to Bangladesh to serve as a volunteer consultant for Inter Pares. "Things were in motion," he says.

Bangladesh, India, Honduras, Brazil, Peru, Nicaragua, Bolivia—each visit strengthened his vocation and his vision until he came up with the concept of Calmeadow, a businessperson's answer to poverty, which he nurtured like a child.

Several blocks east of the gleaming granite building that houses her father's foundation and company, 26-year-old Seanna Connell is taking a break in the basement of the Christian Resource Centre in a subsidized housing development. The brown eyes are just as warm and direct as her father's, but the free spirit burns even brighter. "Last year," she says with a survivor's grin, "I was living below the poverty line."

Seanna's not rebelling against her own good fortune. She's working with homeless men, addicts, pimps, prostitutes and runaways because she has something she wants to give. Something her father speaks of too: "The right to dignity."

For two years Seanna has been teaching art therapy at Toronto drop-in centres. Through paint and paper, she hopes to draw out the resources and self-worth of people who are discouraged, defeated, who don't fit society. The parallel between father and daughter is obvious, but Connell's eldest from his first marriage is her own person.

"Dad always encouraged us to be adventurous and caring," she says. "Six years ago I went to Honduras, and I guess coming back was the hard part. You're hit by what you have." So Seanna looked at what she had and what she could do—and as her father says with unmuted pride, "She's sure not going to get rich doing it, but she's a richer person because of it."

Connell won't take *any* credit for his daughter's caring, saying simply, "If one can be an example, if one can put value in front of people, sometimes these things can happen."

If so, then a lot of things are going to happen, now that Connell is putting the value of giving time and money in front of the whole country. In 1988, he was asked to lead the five-year Imagine campaign, which is inspiring greater generosity in people through outreach programs, speeches, editorials and public-service advertising. Now at the half-way point in the campaign, Connell thinks the message is getting through: more than 200 major Canadian companies have committed to give one percent or more of their pretax profits to worthwhile causes, doubling the existing national average for Canadian corporations. "That may not sound like a lot of companies," says Connell, "but when you look at the dollars they're handling, they represent over a third of corporate giving in the country."

Boosting individuals' generosity is the tougher challenge, as he well knows. "If I've learned anything, changing public behaviour is going to take a lot longer than any five-year line of activities." In the meantime, many charities and their fundraisers, impatient for the public's largesse, are wondering if the well-meaning $9.3 million message is just that—all words, no action. Allan Arlett, former president and chief executive officer of the Centre for Philanthropy, who is now heading a charitable-fundraising consultancy, has heard the grumblings and rejects them. "Imagine isn't based on an airy-fairy idea. The number of companies that have moved to the one-percent corporate-giving level illustrates that. Its purpose is to establish new standards of giving and to raise sights." From there, he says, "it's up to charities to tell people, ' *We* are a vehicle through which you can act.' "

Imagine may rely on words, but it isn't the same old tired pitch. Like Calmeadow, it preaches a pragmatic bottom-line philanthropy: giving is good for the *giver*. If that sounds like self-interest, Connell's all for it. "Because it means that if I'm doing something and I feel I've enriched *my* life for doing it then I'll want to do more."

Connell doesn't like the word "charity." It implies some kind of noblesse oblige, and that's not what's driving him or this new self-interested philanthropy. "I don't want to be seen as someone who would give money away to assuage some internal guilt," he says firmly. "I have money and I enjoy it and I make no apologies." Indeed, he has realized all his material dreams—a gracious home in the city, a country retreat (on whose grounds he has built a tiny bakery, where he bakes his own bread with such entrepreneurial glee that you half expect him to hang out a shingle).

But in that vulnerable period between Conwest and Calmeadow, Connell did contemplate the grand gesture. "Everybody who has money *must*, at one time or another, explore the notion of giving it all away, of grabbing the sackcloth and doing good works for the rest of one's life, with no material possessions whatsoever." But he concluded it would only "make a splash for a few secs. I'm not the Sultan of Brunei," he says, bursting into laughter. "*My* ability to be effective is to leverage *other* people's resources."

That revelation was liberating for Connell, as it will be for the businesspeople who buy into his dream. "If you have money that goes beyond your immediate needs, it is a tremendously creative social tool—and it's imperative we encourage and develop its use in this way."

Spoken like a true social entrepreneur, one who is closing the gap between wealth and poverty by reconciling his own self-interest and philanthropy. He's a happier man for it, according to John Cleghorn, president and chief operating officer of the Royal Bank, who has been a friend of Connell's since they were first year students at McGill. "Back then, Martin was always searching," he says. "Today, he seems to be searching less. He seems to fit his shadow."

Activities

1. Find a section of the essay that summarizes the author's purpose for writing this essay. Be prepared to defend your choice to your classmates.

2. In a journal entry, compare characteristics of Martin Connell with your own characteristics. Identify one characteristic you feel you have in common with him and one you do not share.

3. With a partner, discuss aspects of Connell's character and activities that you most admire. If there is some characteristic you don't admire about him, share your thoughts about that as well.

4. Using this essay as a model, conduct an interview with someone in your school, family, or community whose achievements you admire. The person might be a top student, athlete, a successful business person or community worker, or someone who has gained recognition in their job or hobby. Develop a profile of the person that includes direct quotations from the interview.

5. Obtain from a newspaper or magazine a profile of a prominent personality. Write a summary of the profile that reveals why the person was chosen as the subject of the article.

End of Unit Activities

1. List five things in life that are more important to you than making money and five things that are less important. Compare your list with other members of a group. As a group, make observations about the importance of money in your lives using your lists as reference.

2. Research the meaning of a Horatio Alger story. Write your own Horatio Alger story and share it in a group.

3. Find an article in the business section of the newspaper that you think would be of interest to students your age. In an oral report to your classmates, present a summary of the article and your reasons for believing it would be interesting to them.

4. Divide the class into five groups and assign each group the task of determining how the getting and spending of money is portrayed in one type of television program listed below. Have the groups present their findings. (Not all programs within each category will necessarily present the topic of money the same way.)
   - sitcoms (situation comedies)
   - game shows
   - soap operas
   - dramatic action shows
   - program-length commercials

5. Debate one of the following resolutions:
   - Be it resolved that it is better to be rich and beautiful than to be poor and smart.
   - Be it resolved that nothing that costs only a dollar is worth having.
   - Be it resolved that money is the root of all evil.
   - Be it resolved that the best things in life are free.

6. Write an essay on one of the following topics:
   - the perfect career for me
   - a business person I admire
   - if I had a million dollars

End of Book Activities

1. Identify the audience of one essay in each unit. Use examples from the essays to support your decision about the audience.

2. Identify the tone of one essay in each unit. For each essay, write the title in the centre of a page and create a visual around it that illustrates the tone of the essay.

3. With a partner, discuss which unit was the most memorable to you and explain the reasons for your choice. Then, select one of the following to include in the unit:
   • another essay
   • an essay that you write
   • a photo essay that you create
   • a poem or story

4. Select three essays in the book and decide whether they are primarily subjective or objective in their approach. Rewrite the introductory paragraph of each essay in the approach not used and decide whether the essay might be more persuasive if written that way.

5. Identify the three most memorable essays in the book and try to determine why they are so. Compare your choices with a classmate and try to come up with a list of features that make essays memorable.

6. Find examples of essays in the book written in contrasting styles, such as a descriptive and an argumentative essay, a reflective and an explanatory essay, a subjective and an objective essay, a serious and a humorous essay. Identify why you think the authors chose the styles they did.

7. Examine the essays in the book that are identified as *Controversy Corner*. Using one as a model, write an essay that might be considered controversial about an issue you feel strongly about.

8. With a partner, examine one of the pairs of essays in the book that are identified as *Point/Counterpoint*. Select a topic and then, working alone, write an essay that supports one side of an issue while your partner writes about the other side.

9. Suggest a title and theme for another unit to include in the book. Locate two or three essays to include in such a unit. Have classmates read and evaluate the appropriateness of your choices.

10. Write a letter to an appropriate elected official (local, provincial, or federal) about an issue raised in one of the essays in this book to request more information or to indicate your position on the matter.

Acknowledgements

Every reasonable effort has been made to acquire permission for copyright material used in this book, and to acknowledge all such indebtedness accurately. However, all errors and omissions called to our attention will be corrected in future printings.

Text

Adolescence: Challenges of the Teen Years: by Nick Gallo. From CURRENT HEALTH 2, Oct. 1987. Copyright ©1987 by Weekly Reader Corporation. Reprinted by permission of Current Health. *What's Great About Teenagers:* by David Elkind, Ph.D. From PARENTS magazine, July 1989. Reprinted by permission of the author. *Where the Child Is Father of the Man:* by Paul Fenn. From THE GLOBE AND MAIL, Aug. 22, 1990. Reprinted by permission of the author. *Devils in Disguise:* by Carol Sevitt. From HOMEMAKER'S, Oct. 1990. Reprinted by permission of Homemaker's. *Reasons to Live:* by Sally Armstrong. From CANADIAN LIVING magazine, Mar. 21, 1987. Reprinted by permission of the author. *Lost Among the Girls:* by Rands Richard Cooper. From THE NEW YORK TIMES MAGAZINE, Oct. 30, 1988. Copyright ©1988 by the New York Times Company. Reprinted by permission. *A Place to Stand On:* From HEART OF A STRANGER by Margaret Laurence. Reprinted by permission of the Canadian publishers McClelland & Stewart. *The Thinking Tree:* by Greg Clary. From VICTORIA magazine, July 1990. Reprinted by permission. *Playing Dice With Megadeath:* by Jared Diamond. From DISCOVER magazine. Copyright ©1990 by Discover magazine. Reprinted by permission. *Battle Over Earth's Lesser Creatures:* by Miro Cernetig. From THE GLOBE AND MAIL, July 14, 1990. Reprinted by permission of the Globe and Mail. *Where the Wild Things Are:* by Cathy Spencer. From OMNI. Copyright ©1990 by Omni Publications International, Ltd. Reprinted by permission of Omni. *Do We Need to Use Animals in Research?—Pro:* by Jane McCabe. From NEWSWEEK, Dec. 26, 1988. Reprinted by permission of the author. *Do We Need to Use Animals in Research?— Con:* From NEWSWEEK, Dec. 26, 1988. Copyright ©1988. by Roger Caras. Reprinted by permission of the author and Roberta Pryor Literacy Agency, Inc. *Boutique Gives Dogs a Chance to Dress Up...:* Reprinted by permission of the Canadian Press. *My Heart Soars:* by Dan George. Reprinted by permission of Hancock House. *The Last Wilderness:* From THE LAST WILDERNESS: IMAGES OF THE CANADIAN WILD by David Suzuki. Reprinted by permission of the author. *The Earth Is One Big System:* by Geoffrey Cowley. From NEWSWEEK, Nov. 7, 1988. Copyright ©1988 by Newsweek, Inc. All rights reserved. Reprinted by permission. *Garbage Blues:* by Carrie Buchanan. From CANADIAN GEOGRAPHIC, Feb./Mar. 1988. Reprinted by permission of the author. *Scientific Perspectives on the Greenhouse Effect:* From The George C. Marshall Institute Study "Scientific Perspectives on the Greenhouse Effect," 1989. Reprinted by permission. *Planting the Seeds of a New Tomorrow:* by Amy Willard Cross. From THE GLOBE AND MAIL, Oct. 4, 1990. Reprinted by permission of the author. *This Vast Land That Shapes Us:* by Peter C. Newman. From CANADIAN GEOGRAPHIC, Dec. 1989/Jan. 1990. Reprinted by permission of Canadian Geographic. *The Mysterious North:* From THE MYSTERIOUS NORTH by Pierre Berton. Reprinted by permission of Elsa Franklin, agent. *The Fragile State of the Francosaskois:* by Matthew Fisher. From THE GLOBE AND MAIL, Sept. 15, 1990. Reprinted by permission of the Globe and Mail. *Pride and Prejudice:* by Peter McMartin. From THE VANCOUVER SUN, May 5, 1990. Reprinted by permission of the Vancouver Sun. *A Purple World:* by Richard Wagamese. From THE CALGARY HERALD, June 9, 1991. Reprinted by permission of the Calgary Herald. *I'm Not Racist But...:* by Neil Bissoondath. Copyright ©1989. Reprinted by permission of Lucinda Vardey Agency for the author. *Why Canada Has to Beat Its Literacy Problem:* by June Callwood. From MORE THAN WORDS CAN SAY (McClelland & Stewart). Reprinted by permission of the author. *The Road to a Broader Horizon:* by Laura Robinson. From THE GLOBE AND MAIL, May 28, 1991. Reprinted by permission of the author. *The Common Passion:* From HOME GAME: HOCKEY AND LIFE IN CANADA by Ken Dryden and Roy MacGregor. Reprinted by permission of the Canadian publishers, McClelland & Stewart, Toronto. *Lightning In Your Heart:* From RUNNING RISKS by Angella Issajenko. Copyright ©1990. Reprinted by permission of MacMillan Canada. *The Skier:* by Nancy Dorey. From CONTEST ESSAYS BY CANADIAN STUDENTS. Copyright ©1991 by Holt, Rinehart & Winston of Canada, Ltd. *Team Sports Merely Glorify Violence, Greed:* by Michele Landsberg. From THE TORONTO STAR, Feb. 2, 1991. Reprinted by permission of the Toronto Star, Syndicate. *Integrated Sports: A Question of Fair Play:* Pro—by Helen Lenskyj, Con— by Fran Rider. From CHATELAINE, Feb. 1988. Reprinted by permission of the authors. *Kid's Games:* by Errol Black. From CANADIAN DIMENSION, July/Aug. 1990. Reprinted by permission of Canadian Dimension, Winnipeg. *Young Money: Spending Power of Teens Has Rocketed:* by Lisa Grogan. From THE FINANCIAL POST, Apr. 24, 1989. Reprinted by permission of the Financial Post. *Brands R Us: How Ads Reflect Our Consumer Society:* by Stephen Garey. From MEDIA & VALUES, #51, published by The Center for Media and Values, Los Angeles. Reprinted by permission. *Capitalism Boiled Down:* From THE MORNINGSIDE WORLD OF STUART MCLEAN. Copyright ©1989 by Stuart McLean. Reprinted by permission of Penguin Books Canada. *Shoppers' Heaven:* by Michael Salter. From REPORT ON BUSINESS magazine, June 1989. Reprinted by permission of Report On Business. *Canadian Dreamer:* by Catherine Collins: From IMPERIAL OIL REVIEW, Summer 1991. Reprinted by permission of Imperial Oil Review.